DREAMS AND IMAGES

DREAMS AND IMAGES

AN ANTHOLOGY *of* CATHOLIC POETS

Edited by JOYCE KILMER

CLUNY

Providence, Rhode Island

CLUNY MEDIA EDITION, 2023

This Cluny edition is a republication of the 1917 Boni & Liveright, Inc.,
edition of *Dreams and Images: An Anthology of Catholic Poetry.*

For more information regarding this title
or any other Cluny Media publication,
please write to info@clunymedia.com, or to
Cluny Media, P.O. Box 1664, Providence, RI 02901

VISIT US ONLINE AT WWW.CLUNYMEDIA.COM

Nihil Obstat: ARTHUR J. SCANLAN, S.T.D., *censor librorum*

Imprimatur: FRANCIS J. SPELLMAN, D.D., *Archbishop, New York*
NEW YORK, MAY 2, 1949

Cover design by Clarke & Clarke
Cover image: Anna Ancher, *Sunlight in the Blue Room,*
1891, oil on canvas
Courtesy of Wikimedia Commons

CONTENTS

to REV. JAMES J. DALY, S.J.

ACKNOWLEDGMENTS

For advice and assistance in collecting and arranging these poems, I am grateful to many friends, especially to Mr. T. R. Smith, Miss Caroline Giltinan and Mr. John Bunker. The publishers, editors and authors who have kindly consented to let me use copyright material are numerous and I assure them of my deep sense of obligation. In particular I desire to thank the following publishers for their generous permission to use all that I required from their lists: Charles Scribner's Sons, John Lane Company, Small, Maynard & Company, P. J. Kennedy Sons, Frederick A. Stokes Company, *The Catholic World*, Houghton Mifflin Company, The Encyclopaedia Press, Henry Holt & Company, The Devin-Adair Company, Little, Brown & Company, The Macmillan Company, Elkin Mathews, *The Ave Maria*, Laurence Gomme, and Wilfrid Meynell.

J. K.

❧　☙

INTRODUCTION

This is not a collection of devotional poems. It is not an attempt to rival Orby Shipley's admirable *Carmina Mariana* or any other similar anthology. What I have tried to do is to bring together the poems in English that I like best that were written by Catholics since the middle of the Nineteenth Century. There are in this book poems religious in theme; there are also love-songs and war songs. But I think that it may be called a book of Catholic poems. For a Catholic is not a Catholic only when he prays; he is a Catholic in all the thoughts and actions of his life. And when a Catholic attempts to reflect in words some of the Beauty of which as a poet he is conscious, he cannot be far from prayer and adoration.

The Church has never been without her great poets. And in the nineteenth century there was a splendid renascence of Catholic poetry written in English. It had already begun when Francis Thompson wrote his Essay on Shelley, in which he longed for the bygone days when poetry was "the lesser sister and helpmate of the Church; the minister to the mind, as the Church to the soul." The members of the Pre-Raphaelite Brotherhood were not Catholics, but their movement was related to the renascence of Catholic poetry—it was an attempt to restore to art and letters some of the glory of the days before what is called the Reformation. Coventry Patmore carried the theories of the Pre-Raphaelite Brotherhood to their logical conclusion, as Newman did those of the Tractarians. Coventry Patmore became a Catholic, and found in his Faith his inspiration and his theme. And his disciple Francis Thompson, born to the Faith which Patmore reached by way of the divine adventure of conversion, with art even greater than that of his master, made of the language of Protestant England an instrument of Catholic adoration.

A few of the poets represented in this book were not yet Catholics when they wrote the poems I have quoted. But I do not think that anyone will find fault with me for including Newman and Hawker among the Catholic poets. I am very sorry that the limitations of space have made me exclude many poems dear to me, many poems that are part of the world's literary heritage. There should be many Catholic anthologies.

The poet sees things hidden from other men, but he sees them only in dreams. A poet is (by the very origin of the word) a maker, but a maker of images, not a creator of life. This is a book of reflections of the Beauty which mortal eyes can see only in reflection, a book of dreams of that Truth which one day we shall waking understand. A book of images it is, too, containing representations carved by those who worked by the aid of memory, the strange memory of men living in Faith.

Joyce Kilmer
AUGUST 1917
165TH REGIMENT, CAMP MILLS
MINEOLA, NEW YORK

DREAMS AND IMAGES

OUR LORD AND OUR LADY

By HILAIRE BELLOC

They warned Our Lady for the Child
  That was Our Blessed Lord,
And She took Him into the desert wild,
  Over the camel's ford.

And a long song She sang to Him
  And a short story told:
And She wrapped Him in a woolen cloak
  To keep Him from the cold.

But when Our Lord was grown a man
  The Rich they dragged Him down,
And they crucified Him in Golgotha,
  Out and beyond the Town.

They crucified Him on Calvary,
  Upon an April day;
And because He had been her little Son
  She followed Him all the way.

Our Lady stood beside the Cross,
  A little space apart,
And when She heard Our Lord cry out
  A sword went through Her Heart.

They laid Our Lord in a marble tomb,
  Dead, in a winding sheet.
But Our Lady stands above the world
  With the white Moon at Her feet.

TO THE BALLIOL MEN STILL IN AFRICA

By HILAIRE BELLOC

Years ago when I was at Balliol,
  Balliol men—and I was one—
Swam together in winter rivers,
  Wrestled together under the sun.
And still in the heart of us, Balliol, Balliol,
  Loved already, but hardly known,
Welded us each of us into the others:
  Called a levy and chose her own.

Here is a House that armours a man
  With the eyes of a boy and the heart of a ranger,
And a laughing way in the teeth of the world
  And a holy hunger and thirst for danger:
Balliol made me, Balliol fed me,
  Whatever I had she gave me again:
And the best of Balliol loved and led me,
  God be with you, Balliol men.

I have said it before, and I say it again,
   There was treason done, and a false word spoken,
And England under the dregs of men,
   And bribes about, and a treaty broken:
But angry, lonely, hating it still,
   I wished to be there in spite of the wrong.
My heart was heavy for Cumnor Hill
   And the hammer of galloping all day long.

Galloping outward into the weather,
   Hands a-ready and battle in all:
Words together and wine together
   And song together in Balliol Hall.
Rare and single! Noble and few! …
   Oh! they have wasted you over the sea!
The only brothers ever I knew,
   The men that laughed and quarrelled with me.

.   .   .   .

Balliol made me, Balliol fed me,
   Whatever I had she gave me again;
And the best of Balliol loved and led me,
   God be with you, Balliol men.

THE SOUTH COUNTRY

By Hilaire Belloc

When I am living in the Midlands
  That are sodden and unkind,
I light my lamp in the evening:
  My work is left behind;
And the great hills of the South Country
Come back into my mind.

The great hills of the South Country
  They stand along the sea;
And it's there walking in the high woods
  That I could wish to be,
And the men that were boys when I was a boy
Walking along with me.

The men that live in North England
  I saw them for a day:
Their hearts are set upon the waste fells,
  Their skies are fast and grey;
From their castle-walls a man may see;
  The mountains far away.
The men that live in West England

They see the Severn strong,
  A-rolling on rough water brown,
Light aspen leaves along.

They have the secret of the Rocks,
And the oldest kind of song.

But the men that live in the South Country
   Are the kindest and most wise,
They get their laughter from the loud surf,
   And the faith in their happy eyes
Comes surely from our Sister the Spring
   When over the sea she flies;
The violets suddenly bloom at her feet,
   She blesses us with surprise.

I never get between the pines
   But I smell the Sussex air;
Nor I never come on a belt of sand
   But my home is there.
And along the sky the line of Downs
   So noble and so bare.

A lost thing could I never find,
   Nor a broken thing mend:
And I fear I shall be all alone
   When I get towards the end.
Who will there be to comfort me
   Or who will be my friend?

I will gather and carefully make my friends
   Of the men of the Sussex Weald,
They watch the stars from silent folds,

They stiffly plough the field.
By them and the God of the South Country
My poor soul shall be healed.

If I ever become a rich man,
 Or if ever I grow to be old,
I will build a house with deep thatch
 To shelter me from the cold,
And there shall the Sussex songs be sung
 And the story of Sussex told.

I will hold my house in the high wood
 Within a walk of the sea,
And the men that were boys when I was a boy
 Shall sit and drink with me.

THE EARLY MORNING

By HILAIRE BELLOC

The moon on the one hand, the dawn on the other:
The moon is my sister, the dawn is my brother,
The moon on my left and the dawn on my right.
My brother, good morning: my sister, good night.

THE PROPHET LOST IN THE HILLS AT EVENING

By HILAIRE BELLOC

Strong God which made the topmost stars
  To circulate and keep their course,
Remember me; whom all the bars
  Of sense and dreadful fate enforce.

Above me in your heights and tall,
  Impassable the summits freeze,
Below the haunted waters call
  Impassable beyond the trees.

I hunger and I have no bread.
  My gourd is empty of the wine.
Surely the footsteps of the dead
  Are shuffling softly close to mine!

It darkens. I have lost the ford.
  There is a change on all things made.
The rocks have evil faces, Lord,
  And I am awfully afraid.

Remember me! the Voids of Hell
  Expand enormous all around.
Strong friend of souls, Emmanuel,
  Redeem me from accursed ground.

The long descent of wasted days,
  To these at last have led me down;
Remember that I filled with praise
The meaningless and doubtful ways
  That lead to an eternal town.

I challenged and I kept the Faith,
  The bleeding path alone I trod;
It darkens. Stand about my wraith,
  And harbour me—almighty God!

THE BIRDS

By HILAIRE BELLOC

When Jesus Christ was four years old,
The angels brought Him toys of gold,
Which no man ever had bought or sold.

And yet with these He would not play.
He made Him small fowl out of clay,
And blessed them till they flew away:
  Tu creasti Domine.

Jesus Christ, Thou child so wise,
Bless mine hands and fill mine eyes,
And bring my soul to Paradise.

COURTESY

By HILAIRE BELLOC

Of Courtesy, it is much less
Than Courage of Heart or Holiness,
Yet in my Walks it seems to me
That the Grace of God is in Courtesy.

On Monks I did in Storrington fall,
They took me straight into their Hall;
I saw Three Pictures on a wall,
And Courtesy was in them all.

The first Annunciation;
The second the Visitation;
The third the Consolation,
Of God that was Our Lady's Son.

The first was of Saint Gabriel;
On Wings a-flame from Heaven he fell;
And as he went upon one knee
He shone with Heavenly Courtesy.

Our Lady out of Nazareth rode—
It was her month of heavy load;
Yet was Her face both great and kind,
For Courtesy was in Her Mind.

The third it was our Little Lord,
Whom all the Kings in arms adored;
He was so small you could not see
His large intent of Courtesy.

Our Lord, that was Our Lady's Son,
Go bless you, People, one by one;
My Rhyme is written, my work is done.

NOEL

By HILAIRE BELLOC

I.

On a winter's night long time ago
  (*The bells ring loud and the bells ring low*),
When high howled wind, and down fell snow
  (Carillon, Carilla).
Saint Joseph he and Notre Dame,
Riding on an ass, full weary came
From Nazareth into Bethlehem,
  And the small child Jesus smile on you.

II.

And Bethlehem inn they stood before
  (*The bells ring less and the bells ring more*),
The landlord bade them begone from his door

(Carillon, Carilla).
"Poor folk" (says he), "must lie where they may,
For the Duke of Jewry comes this way,
With all his train on a Christmas Day."
    And the small child Jesus smile on you.

III.

Poor folk that may my carol hear
    (*The bells ring single and the bells ring clear*),
See! God's one child had hardest cheer!
    (Carillon, Carilla).
Men grown hard on a Christmas morn;
The dumb beast by and a babe forlorn.
It was very, very cold when our Lord was born.
    And the small child Jesus smile on you.

IV.

Now these were Jews as Jews may be
    (*The bells ring merry and the bells ring free*).
But Christian men in a band are we
    (Carillon, Carilla).
Empty we go, and ill be-dight,
Singing Noel on a Winter's night.
Give us to sup by the warm firelight,
    And the small child Jesus smile on you.

AFTER A RETREAT

By ROBERT HUGH BENSON

What hast thou learnt today?
Hast thou sounded awful mysteries,
Hast pierced the veiléd skies,
Climbed to the feet of God,
Trodden where saints have trod,
Fathomed the heights above?
   Nay,
This only have I learnt, that God is love.

What hast thou heard today?
Hast heard the Angel-trumpets cry,
And rippling harps reply;
  Heard from the Throne of flame
Whence God incarnate came
Some thund'rous message roll?
   Nay,
This have I heard, His voice within my soul.

What hast thou felt today?
The pinions of the Angel-guide
That standeth at thy side
In rapturous ardours beat,
Glowing, from head to feet,
In ecstasy divine?

Nay,
This only have I felt, Christ's hand in mine.

THE TERESIAN CONTEMPLATIVE

By ROBERT HUGH BENSON

She moves in tumult; round her lies
   The silence of the world of grace;
The twilight of our mysteries
   Shines like high noonday on her face;
Our piteous guesses, dim with fears,
She touches, handles, sees, and hears.

In her all longings mix and meet;
   Dumb souls through her are eloquent;
She feels the world beneath her feet
   Thrill in a passionate intent;
Through her our tides of feeling roll
And find their God within her soul.

Her faith and awful Face of God
   Brightens and blinds with utter light;
Her footsteps fall where late He trod;
   She sinks in roaring voids of night;
Cries to her Lord in black despair,
And knows, yet knows not, He is there.

A willing sacrifice she takes
  The burden of our fall within;
Holy she stands; while on her breaks
  The lightning of the wrath of sin;
She drinks her Saviour's cup of pain,
And, one with Jesus, thirsts again.

HOW SHALL I BUILD

By WILFRID SCAWEN BLUNT

How shall I build my temple to the Lord,
  Unworthy I, who am thus foul of heart?
How shall I worship who no traitor word
  Know but of love to play a suppliant's part?
How shall I pray, whose soul is as a mart,
  For thoughts unclean, whose tongue is as a sword
Even for those it loves, to wound and smart?
  Behold how little I can help Thee, Lord.

The Temple I would build should be all white,
  Each stone the record of a blameless day;
The souls that entered there should walk in light,
  Clothed in high chastity and wisely gay.
Lord, here is darkness. Yet this heart unwise,
  Bruised in Thy service, take in sacrifice.

SONG

By WILFRID SCAWEN BLUNT

O fly not, Pleasure, pleasant-hearted Pleasure;
　Fold me thy wings, I prithee, yet and stay:
　　For my heart no measure
　　Knows, or other treasure
　To buy a garland for my love today.

And thou, too, Sorrow, tender-hearted Sorrow,
　Thou gray-eyed mourner, fly not yet away:
　　For I fain would borrow
　　Thy sad weeds tomorrow,
　To make a mourning for love's yesterday.

The voice of Pity, Time's divine dear Pity,
　Moved me to tears: I dared not say them nay,
　　But passed forth from the city,
　　Making thus my ditty
　Of fair love lost forever and a day.

THE DESOLATE CITY

By WILFRID SCAWEN BLUNT

Dark to me is the earth. Dark to me are the heavens.
  Where is she that I loved, the woman with eyes like stars?
Desolate are the streets. Desolate is the city.
  A city taken by storm, where none are left but the slain.

Sadly I rose at dawn, undid the latch of my shutters,
  Thinking to let in light, but I only let in love.
Birds in the boughs were awake; I listen'd to their chaunting;
  Each one sang to his love; only I was alone.

This, I said in my heart, is the hour of life and pleasure.
  Now each creature on earth has his joy, and lives in the sun,
Each in another's eyes finds light, the light of compassion,
  This is the moment of pity, this is the moment of love.
Speak, O desolate city! Speak, O silence in sadness!
  Where is she that loved in my strength, that spoke to
    my soul?
Where are those passionate eyes that appealed to my eyes
  in passion?
  Where is the mouth that kiss'd me, the breast that I laid to
    my own?

Speak, thou soul of my soul, for rage in my heart is kindled.
  Tell me, where didst thou flee in the day of destruction
    and fear?

See, my arms enfold thee, enfolding thus all heaven,
  See, my desire is fulfilled in thee, for it fills the earth.

Thus in my grief I lamented. Then turned I from the window,
  Turn'd to the stair, and the open door, and the empty street,
Crying aloud in my grief, for there was none to chide me,
  None to mock my weakness, none to behold my tears.

Groping I went, as blind. I sought her house, my beloved's.
  There I stopp'd at the silent door, and listen'd and tried
    the latch.
Love, I cried, dost thou slumber? This is no hour for slumber,
  This is the hour of love, and love I bring in my hand.

I knew the house with its windows barr'd, and its leafless
  fig-tree,
  Climbing round by the doorstep, the only one in the street;
I knew where my hope had climbed to its goal and there
  encircled,
  All those desolate walls once held, my beloved's heart.

There in my grief she consoled me. She loved when I
  loved not.
  She put her hand in my hand, and set her lips to my lips.
She told me all her pain and show'd me all her trouble.
  I, like a fool, scarce heard, hardly return'd her kiss.

Love, thy eyes were like torches. They changed as I
  beheld them.

Love, thy lips were like gems, the seal thou settest on my life.
Love, if I loved not then, behold this hour thy vengeance;
This is the fruit of thy love and thee, the unwise grown wise.

Weeping strangled my voice. I call'd out, but none answered;
Blindly the windows gazed back at me, dumbly the door;
She whom I love, who loved me, look'd not on my yearning,
Gave me no more her hands to kiss, show'd me no more
her soul.

Therefore the earth is dark to me, the sunlight blackness,
Therefore I go in tears and alone, by night and day;
Therefore I find my love in heaven, no light, no beauty,
A heaven taken by storm, where none are left but the slain!

A CHRISTMAS SONG

By TERESA BRAYTON

O Lord, as You lay so soft and white,
  A Babe in a manger stall,
With the big star flashing across the night,
  Did you know and pity us all?
Did the wee hands, close as a rosebud curled,
  With the call of their mission ache,
To be out and saving a weary world
  For Your merciful Father's sake?

Did You hear the cries of the groping blind,
  The woe of the leper's prayer,
The surging sorrow of all mankind,
  As You lay by Your Mother there?
Beyond the shepherds, low bending down,
  The long, long road did You see
That led from peaceful Bethlehem town
  To the summit of Calvary?

The world grown weary of wasting strife,
  Had called for the Christ to rise;
For sin had poisoned the springs of life
  And only the dead were wise.
But, wrapped in a dream of scornful pride,
  Too high were its eyes to see
A Child, foredoomed to be crucified,
  On a peasant Mother's knee.

But, while the heavens with glad acclaim
  Sang out the tale of Your birth,
A mystic echo of comfort came
  To the desolate souls of earth.
For the thrill of a slowly turning tide
  Was felt in that grey daybreak,
As if God, the Father, had sanctified
  All sorrow for One Man's sake.

O Child of the Promise! Lord of Love!
  O Master of all the earth!

While the angels are singing their songs above,
  We bring our gifts to Your birth.
Just the blind man's cry, and the lame man's pace,
  And the leper's pitiful call;
On these, over infinite fields of space,
  Look down, for You know them all.

LIKE ONE I KNOW

By NANCY CAMPBELL

Little Christ was good, and lay
Sleeping, smiling in the hay;
Never made the cows round eyes
Open wider at His cries;
Never when the night was dim,
Startled guardian Seraphim,
Who above Him in the beams
Kept their watch round His white dreams;
Let the rustling brown mice creep
Undisturbed about His sleep.
Yet if it had not been so—
Had He been like one I know,
Fought with little fumbling hands,
Kicked inside His swaddling bands,
Puckered wilful crimsoning face—
Mary Mother, full of grace,

At that little naughty thing,
Still had been a-worshipping.

MEA CULPA

By ETHNA CARBERY

Be pitiful, my God!
  No hard-won gifts I bring—
But empty, pleading hands
  To Thee at evening.

Spring came, white-browed and young,
  I, too, was young with Spring.
There was a blue, blue heaven
  Above a skylark's wing.

Youth is the time for joy,
  I cried, it is not meet
To mount the heights of toil
  With child-soft feet.

When Summer walked the land
  In Passion's red arrayed,
Under green sweeping boughs
  My couch I made.

The noon-tide heat was sore,
  I slept the Summer through;
An angel waked me—"Thou
  Hast work to do."

I rose and saw the sheaves
  Upstanding in a row;
The reapers sang Thy praise
  While passing to and fro.

My hands were soft with ease,
  Long were the Autumn hours;
I left the ripened sheaves
  For poppy-flowers.

But lo! now Winter glooms,
  And gray is in my hair,
Whither has flown the world
  I found so fair?

My patient God, forgive!
  Praying Thy pardon sweet
I lay a lonely heart
  Before Thy feet.

IN TIR-NA'N-OG

By ETHNA CARBERY

In Tir-na'n-Og,
In Tir-na'n-Og,
Summer and spring go hand in hand, and in the radiant
  weather
Brown autumn leaves and winter snow come floating
  down together.

In Tir-na'n-Og,
In Tir-na'n-Og,
The sagans sway this way and that, the twisted fern uncloses,
The quicken-berry hides its red above the tender roses.

In Tir-na'n-Og,
In Tir-na'n-Og,
The blackbird lilts, the robin chirps, the linnet wearies never,
They pipe to dancing feet of *Sidhe* and thus shall pipe forever.

In Tir-na'n-Og,
In Tir-na'n-Og,
All in a drift of apple blooms my true love there is roaming,
He will not come although I pray from dawning until
  gloaming.

In Tir-na'n-Og,
In Tir-na'n-Og,

The *Sidhe* desired my Heart's Delight, they lured him
   from my keeping,
He stepped within a fairy ring while all the world
   was sleeping.

   In Tir-na'n-Og,
   In Tir-na'n-Og,
He hath forgotten hill and glen where misty shadows gather,
The bleating of the mountain sheep, the cabin of his father.

   In Tir-na'n-Og,
   In Tir-na'n-Og,
He wanders in a happy dream thro' scented golden hours,
He flutes, to woo a fairy love, knee deep in fairy flowers.

   In Tir-na'n-Og,
   In Tir-na'n-Og,
No memory hath he of my face, no sorrow for my sorrow,
My flax is spun, my wheel is hushed, and so I wait the morrow.

LADY DAY IN IRELAND

By P. J. CARROLL, C.S.C.

Through the long August day, mantled blue with a sky of
   Our Lady,

They are there at the well from the dawn till the sea birds
   go home;
And the trees bending down with broad leaves offer spots
   that are shady,
     Where the heart is at rest, sighing prayers till the shadows
     are come.

The brown beads and the crucifix pass in procession
   through fingers
     That are pale as the snow or are hardened from labor
     and pain.
In each *Ave* they whisper the deep Celtic tenderness lingers,
     Like a sweet phrase in song that is echoed and echoed again.

Marching down the white road with the sun in the noon of
   his splendor
     Are the children, with joy in the blue of their innocent eyes;
In their hearts is a song, breaking forth into words that
   are tender,
     Unto her with the gold of the stars and the blue of the skies.

In the still summer air there's a chorus of minstrelsy
   breaking,
     There are flashes of gold with a flutter and waving
     of wings:
Mary's birds are they, come with the dawn, all the green
   woods forsaking,
     Every heart in them breaking for love with the message
     it brings.

Through the calm August day, with Our Lady's blue sky far
above them,
And beyond the grey mountains where slumbers the Irish
green sea,
There they speak to her, weep while they pray to her, beg
her to love them,
Till beyond the bright stars where their home and their
treasure shall be.

ST. PATRICK'S TREASURE

By P. J. CARROLL, C.S.C.

Called son by many lands,
Thou art a father unto one.
Of all these mothers claiming thee,
By honored titles naming thee,

We ask: Where is thy priceless birthright gone?
That blessed faith of thine,
They mothering thee have sold.
But she, thy daughter dutiful,
Has kept thy treasure beautiful
Through many sorrows in her heart of gold.

THE SPOUSE OF CHRIST

By D. A. CASEY

He came to her from out eternal years,
A smile upon His lips, a tender smile
That, somehow, spoke of partings and of tears.

'Twas eventide, and silence brooded low
On earth and sky—the hour when haunting fears
Of mystery pursue us as we go.

Strange, mystic shadows filled the temple dim,
But on the Golden Door the ruby glow
Spoke orisons more sweet than vesper hymn.

No human accents voiced His gentle call,
No crashing thunderbolts did wait on Him,
As when of old He deigned to summon Saul.

But heart did speak to heart, an unseen chord
In Love's own scale did sweetly rise and fall;
Nor questioned she, but meekly answered "Lord!"

Tonight some household counts a vacant chair,
But far on high Christ portions the reward,
A hundred-fold for each poor human care.

CHRIST THE COMRADE

By PADRAIC COLUM

Christ, by Thine own darkened hour
   Live within my heart and brain!
   Let my hands not slip the rein.

Ah, how long ago it is
   Since a comrade rode with me!
   Now a moment let me see

Thyself, lonely in the dark,
Perfect, without wound or mark.

AN OLD WOMAN OF THE ROADS

By PADRAIC COLUM

Oh, to have a little house,
   To own the hearth and stool and all—
The heaped-up sods upon the fire,
   The pile of turf against the wall!

To have a clock with weights and chains,
   And pendulum swinging up and down!
A dresser filled with shining delph,
   Speckled and white and blue and brown!

I could be busy all the day
  Clearing and sweeping hearth and floor,
And fixing on their shelf again
  My white and blue speckled store.

I could be quiet there at night
  Beside the fire and by myself,
Sure of a bed, and loth to leave
  The ticking clock and shining delph.

Och! but I'm weary of mist and dark,
  And roads where there's never a house or bush,
And tired I am of bog and road,
  And the crying wind and the lonesome hush.

And I am praying to God on high,
  And I am praying Him night and day,
For a little house—a house of my own—
  Out of the wind's and the rain's way.

THE HEAVIEST CROSS OF ALL

By KATHERINE ELEANOR CONWAY

I've borne full many a sorrow, I've suffered many a loss—
But now, with a strange, new anguish, I carry this last
  dread cross;

For of this be sure, my dearest, whatever thy life befall,
The cross that our own hands fashion is the heaviest cross
    of all.

Heavy and hard I made it in the days of my fair strong youth,
Veiling mine eyes from the blessed light, and closing my
    heart to truth.
Pity me, Lord, whose mercy passeth my wildest thought,
For I never dreamed of the bitter end of the work my hands
    had wrought!

In the sweet morn's flush and fragrance I wandered o'er
    dewy meadows,
And I hid from the fervid noontide glow in the cool green
    woodland shadows;
And I never recked, as I sang aloud in my wilful, selfish glee,
Of the mighty woe that was drawing nigh to darken the
    world for me.

But it came at last, my dearest—what need to tell thee how?
Mayst never know of the wild, wild woe that my heart is
    bearing now!
Over my summer's glory crept a damp and chilling shade,
And I staggered under the heavy cross that my sinful hands
    had made.

I go where the shadows deepen, and the end seems far off yet—
God keep thee safe from the sharing of this woeful late regret!
For of this be sure, my dearest, whatever thy life befall,

The crosses we make for ourselves, alas! are the heaviest
ones of all.

SATURNINUS

By KATHERINE ELEANOR CONWAY

He might have won the highest guerdon that heaven to earth
can give,
For whoso falleth for justice—dying, he yet shall live.
He might have left us his memory to flame as a beacon light,
When clouds of the false world's raising shut the stars of
heaven from sight.

He might have left us his name to ring in our triumph song
When we stand, as we'll stand at tomorrow's dawn, by the
grave of a world-old wrong.

For he gave thee, O mother of valiant sons, thou fair, and
sore oppressed,
The love of his youth and his manhood's choice—first-fruits
of his life, and best.

Thine were throb of his heart and thought of his brain and
toil of his strong right hand;
For thee he braved scorn and reviling, and loss of gold
and land,

Threat and lure and false-hearted friend, and blight of a
　broken word—
Terrors of night and delay of light—prison and rack
　and sword.

For thee he bade death defiance—till the heavens opened
　wide,
And his face grew bright with reflex of light from the face of
　the Crucified.

And his crown was in sight and his palm in reach and his
　glory all but won,
And then—he failed—God help us! with the worst of dying
　done.

Only to die on the treacherous down by the hands of the
　tempters spread—
Nay, nay—make way for the strangers! we have no right in
　the dead.

But oh, for the beacon quenched, that we dreamed would
　kindle and flame!
And oh, for the standard smirched and shamed, and the
　name we dare not name!

Over the lonesome grave the shadows gather fast;
Only the mother, like God, forgives, and comforts her
　heart with the past.

DREAMING OF CITIES DEAD

By ELEANOR ROGERS COX

Dreaming of cities dead,
Of bright Queens vanished,
Of kings whose names were but as seed wind-blown
E'en when white Patrick's voice shook Tara's throne,
My way along the great world-street I tread,
And keep the rites of Beauty lost, alone.

Cairns level with the dust—
Names dim with Time's dull rust—
Afar they sleep on many a wind-swept hill,
The beautiful, the strong of heart and will—
On whose pale dreams no sunrise joy shall burst,
No harper's song shall pierce with battle-thrill.

Long from their purpled heights,
Their reign of high delights,
The Queens have wended down Death's mildewed stair,
Leaving a scent of lilies on the air,
To gladden Earth through all her days and nights,
That once she cherished anything so fair.

DEATH OF CUCHULAIN

By ELEANOR ROGERS COX

Silent are the singers in the purple halls of Emain,
  Silent all the harp-strings untouched of any hand,
Wan as twilight roses the radiant, royal women,
  Black unto the hearthstone the erstwhile flaming brand.

Inward far from ocean the storm's white birds are flying,
  Darting, like dim wraith flames across the falling night.
Winds like a *caoine* through the quicken groves are sighing,
  On no lip is laughter, in no heart delight.

For thitherwards witch-wafted athwart the sundering spaces,
  Lo, a word doom-freighted unto Conchubar has come,
Whispering of one who in far-off, hostile places
  Strikes a last defending blow for king and home.

And the King pacing lone in his place of High Decision,
  Gazing with rapt eyes on that far-flung battle-plain,
Through the red rains rising beholds with startled vision
  Sight such as man's eye shall not see again.

For one there is dying, of his foes at last outnumbered,
  One whose soul a sword was, shaped by God's own hand,
One who guarded Ulaidh when all her knighthood
  slumbered,
  Prone beneath the curse laid of old upon the land.

And dying so, alone, of all mortal aid forsaken,
  Dead his peerless war steeds, dead his charioteer,
Yet the high splendor of his spirit all unshaken,
  Shines morning-bright through the Death-mists drawing near.

And radiant round his brow yet the hero-flame is gleaming,
  And firm yet his footstep upon the reddened sod,
As with sword uplifted towards the day's last beaming,
  Forth goes the spirit of Cuchulain unto God.

Leaving to his land and the Celtic race forever
  That which shall not fail them throughout the fading years,
Heritage of faith unchanged, of fear-undimmed endeavor,
  And a quenchless laughter ringing down the edge of hostile
  spears.

GODS AND HEROES OF THE GAEL

By Eleanor Rogers Cox

Forth in shining phalanx marching from the shrouding mists
  of time,
  Bright the sunlight on their foreheads, bright upon their
    golden mail,
Lords of beauty, lords of valor, lords of Earth's unconquered
  prime,
  Come the gods, the kings, the heroes of the Gael.

Lugh, the splendor of whose shining lit the forest and the fen,
  He whose smile at first illuming all the shadow-haunted space
Of the vast, primeval ranges, death-engirdled, shunned of men,
  Over virgin seas to Erin led our race.

Mananaan, great lord of Ocean—he whose fair domain
  outspread
    Wheresoever tides foam-flowered to the moon's high
    mandate move,
Aengus, clothed in youth immortal, on immortal ardors fed,
  Who of old in golden Brugh reigned lord of Love.

And his name a knightly pennon on the ramparts of the world,
  And his fame a fire unfailing on Time's utmost purple height,
Erin's peerless gage of courage to the vaunting ages hurled—
  Sunward evermore Cuchulain holds his flight.

They are coming with the silver speech of Erin on their lips;
  The speech that once of all the mighty Celtic race made kin,
They are coming with the laughter that has known no
  age-eclipse,
    They are coming with the songs beloved of Finn.

Yea, with gifts regenerating to all men of women born—
  Flame of courage that shall fade not, flame of truth that
    shall not fail,
To the music of a thousand harps they're marching through
  the Morn,
    Deathless gods and kings and heroes of the Gael!

AT BENEDICTION

By Eleanor Rogers Cox

Joy, beauty, awe, supremest worship blending
  In one long breath of perfect ecstasy,
Song from our hearts to God's own Heart ascending,
  The mortal merged in immortality.
There, veiled beneath that sacramental whiteness,
  The wonder that all wonders doth transcend,
The Word that kindled chaos into brightness,
  Our Lord, our God, our origin, our end.
Light, light, a sea of light, unshored, supernal,
  Is all about our finite being spread,
Deep, soundless waves of harmonies eternal
  Their balm celestial on our spirits shed.
O Source of Life! O Fount of waters living!
  O Love, to whom all powers of mind and soul,
We give, and find again within the giving,
  Of Thee renewed, made consecrate and whole.

PRIMROSE HILL

By Olive Custance

Wild heart in me that frets and grieves,
Imprisoned here against your will...

Sad heart that dreams of rainbow wings...
See! I have found some golden things!
The poplar trees on Primrose Hill
With all their shining play of leaves...
And London like a silver bride,
That will not put her veil aside!

Proud London like a painted Queen,
Whose crown is heavy on her head...
City of sorrow and desire,
Under a sky of opal fire,
Amber and amethyst and red...
And how divine the day has been!
For every dawn God builds again
This world of beauty and of pain....

Wild heart that hungers for delight,
Imprisoned here against your will;
Sad heart, so eager to be gay!
Loving earth's lovely things...the play
Of wind and leaves on Primrose Hill...
Or London dreaming of the night...
Adventurous heart, on beauty bent,
That only Heaven could quite content!

TWILIGHT

By OLIVE CUSTANCE

Spirit of Twilight, through your folded wings
   I catch a glimpse of your averted face,
And rapturous on a sudden, my soul sings
   "Is not this common earth a holy place?"
Spirit of Twilight, you are like a song
   That sleeps, and waits a singer—like a hymn
That God finds lovely and keeps near Him long,
   Till it is choired by aureoled cherubim.
Spirit of Twilight, in the golden gloom
   Of dreamland dim I sought you, and I found
A woman sitting in a silent room
   Full of white flowers that moved and made no sound.
These white flowers were the thoughts you bring to all,
   And the room's name is Mystery where you sit,
Woman whom we call Twilight, when night's pall
   You lift across our Earth to cover it.

TO A THRUSH

By T. A. DALY

Sing clear, O! throstle,
Thou golden-tongued apostle

And little brown-frocked brother
    Of the loved Assisian!
Sing courage to the mother,
    Sing strength into the man,
For they, who in another May
    Trod Hope's scant wine from grapes of pain,
Have tasted in thy song today
    The bitter-sweet red lees again.
To them in whose sad May-time thou
Sang'st comfort from thy maple bough,
    To tinge the presaged dole with sweet,
O! prophet then, be prophet now
    And paraclete!

That fateful May! The pregnant vernal night
  Was throbbing with the first faint pangs of day,
The while with ordered urge toward life and light,
    Earth-atoms countless groped their destined way;
    And one full-winged to fret
    Its tender oubliette,
The warding mother-heart above it woke,
  Darkling she lay in doubt, then, sudden wise,
Whispered her husband's drowsy ear and broke
  The estranging seal of slumber from his eyes:
  "My hour is nigh: arise!"

Already, when, with arms for comfort linked,
  The lovers at an eastward window stood,
The rosy day, in cloudy swaddlings, blinked

Through misty green new-fledged in Wister Wood.
    Breathless upon this birth
    The still-entranced earth
Seemed brooding, motionless in windless space.
    Then rose thy priestly chant, O! holy bird!
And heaven and earth were quickened with its grace;
    To tears two wedded souls were moved who heard,
    And one, unborn, was stirred!

O! Comforter, enough that from thy green
    Hid tabernacle in the wood's recess
To those care-haunted lovers thou, unseen,
    Should'st send thy flame-tipped song to cheer and bless.
      Enough for them to hear
      And feel thy presence near;
And yet when he, regardful of her ease,
    Had led her back by brightening hall and stair
To her own chamber's quietude and peace,
    One maple-bowered window shook with rare,
    Sweet song—and thou wert there!

Hunter of souls! the loving chase so nigh
    Those spirits twain had never come before.
They saw the sacred flame within thine eye;
    To them the maple's depths quick glory wore,
      As though God's hand had lit
      His altar-fire in it,
And made a fane, of virgin verdure pleached,
    Wherefrom thou might'st in numbers musical

Expound the age-sweet words thy Francis preached
  To thee and thine, of God's benignant thrall
  That broodeth over all.

And they, athirst for comfort, sipped thy song,
  But drank not yet thy deeper homily.
Not yet, but when parturient pangs grew strong,
  And from its cell the young soul struggled free—
    A new joy, trailing grief,
    A little crumpled leaf,
Blighted before it burgeoned from the stem—
  Thou, as the fabled robin to the rood,
Wert minister of charity to them;
  And from the shadows of sad parenthood
  They heard and understood.

Makes God one soul a lure for snaring three?
  Ah! surely; so this nursling of the nest,
This teen-touched joy, ere birth anoint of thee,
  Yet bears thy chrismal music in her breast.
    Five Mays have come and sped
    Above her sunny head,
And still the happy song abides in her.
  For though on maimed limbs the body creeps,
It doth a spirit house whose pinions stir
  Familiarly the far cerulean steeps
  Where God His mansion keeps.

So come, O! throstle,
  Thou golden-tongued apostle
And little brown-frocked brother
  Of the loved Assisian!
Sing courage to the mother,
  Sing strength into the man,
That she who in another May
  Came out of heaven, trailing care,
May never know that sometimes gray
  Earth's roof is and its cupboards bare.
To them in whose sad May-time thou
Sang'st comfort and thy maple bough,
  To tinge the presaged dole with sweet,
O! prophet then, be prophet now
  And paraclete!

TO A PLAIN SWEETHEART

By T. A. DALY

I love thee, dear, for what thou art,
  Nor would I wish thee otherwise,
For when thy lashes lift apart
  I read, deep-mirrored in thine eyes,
The glory of a modest heart.

Wert thou as fair as thou art good,
　It were not given to any man,
With daring eyes of flesh and blood,
　To look thee in the face and scan
The splendor of thy womanhood.

TO A ROBIN

By T. A. DALY

I heard thee, joyous votary,
　Pour forth thy heart in one
Sweet simple strain of melody
　To greet the rising sun,
When he across the morning's verge his first faint flare
　had flung
And found the crimson of thy breast the whisp'ring
　leaves among,
　　In thine own tree
　　Which sheltered thee,
　Thy mate, thy nest, thy young.

I marked thee, sorrow's votary,
　When in the noon of day
Young vandals stormed thy sacred tree
　And bore thine all away;
The notes of grief that rent thy breast touched kindred

chords in mine,
For memories of other days, though slumbering
   still confine
      In mine own heart
      The bitter smart
   Of sorrow such as thine.

I hear thee now, sweet votary,
   Beside thy ruined nest,
Lift up thy flood of melody
   Against the crimsoned west,
Forgetful of all else in this, thy one sweet joyous strain.
I thank thee for this ecstasy of my remembered pain;
      Thou liftest up
      My sorrow's cup
   To sweeten it again.

THE POET

By T. A. DALY

The truest poet is not one
Whose golden fancies fuse and run
To moulded phrases, crusted o'er
With flashing gems of metaphor;
Whose art, responsive to his will,
Makes voluble the thoughts that fill

The cultured windings of his brain,
Yet takes no soundings of the pain,
The joy, the yearnings of the heart
Untrammeled by the bonds of art,
O! poet truer far than he
Is such a one as you may be,
When in the quiet night you keep
Mute vigil on the marge of sleep.

If then, with beating heart, you mark
God's nearer presence in the dark,
And musing on the wondrous ways
Of Him who numbers all your days,
Pay tribute to Him with your tears
For joys, for sorrows, hopes and fears
Which he has blessed and given to you,
You are the poet, great and true.
For there are songs within the heart
Whose perfect melody no art
Can teach the tongue of man to phrase.
These are the songs His poets raise,
When in the night they keep
Mute vigil on the marge of sleep.

OCTOBER

By T. A. DALY

Come, forsake your city street!
Come to God's own fields and meet
    October.
Not the lean, unkempt and brown
Counterfeit that haunts the town,
Pointing, like a thing of gloom,
At dead summer in her tomb;
Reading in each fallen leaf
Nothing but regret and grief.
Come out, where, beneath the blue,
You may frolic with the true
    October.

Call his name and mark the sound,
Opulent and full and round:
    "October."
Come, and gather from his hand
Lavish largesse of the land;
Read in his prophetic eyes,
Clear as skies of paradise,
Not of summer days that died,
But of summer fructified!
Hear, O soul, his message sweet.
Come to God's own fields and meet
    October.

SORROW

By Aubrey De Vere

Count each affliction, whether light or grave,
  God's messenger sent down to thee; do thou
With courtesy receive him; rise and bow;
  And, ere his shadow pass thy threshold, crave
Permission first His heavenly feet to lave;
  Then lay before Him all thou hast; allow
No cloud or passion to usurp thy brow,
  Or mar thy hospitality; no wave
Of mortal tumult to obliterate
  Thy soul's marmoreal calmness. Grief should be
Like joy, majestic, equable, sedate;
  Confirming, cleansing, raising, making free;
Strong to consume small troubles; to commend
  Great thoughts, grave thoughts, thoughts lasting to the end.

HUMAN LIFE

By Aubrey De Vere

Sad is our youth, for it is ever going,
  Crumbling away beneath our very feet;
Sad is our life, for onward it is flowing,
  In current unperceived because so fleet;

Sad are our hopes, for they were sweet in sowing,
But tares, self-sown, have overtopped the wheat;
Sad are our joys, for they were sweet in blowing;
And still, O still, their dying breath is sweet;
And sweet is youth, although it hath bereft us
Of that which made our childhood sweeter still;
And sweeter our life's decline, for it hath left us
A nearer Good to cure an older Ill;
And sweet are all things, when we learn to prize them
Not for their sake, but His who grants them or denies them.

CARDINAL MANNING

By AUBREY DE VERE

I learn'd his greatness first at Lavington:
The moon had early sought her bed of brine,
But we discours'd till now each starry sign
Had sunk: our theme was one and one alone:
"Two minds supreme," he said, "our earth has known;
One sang in science; one served God in song;
Aquinas—Dante." Slowly in me grew strong
A thought, "These two great minds in him are one;
'Lord, what shall this man do?'" Later at Rome
Beside the dust of Peter and of Paul
Eight hundred mitred sires of Christendom
In Council sat. I mark'd him 'mid them all;

I thought of that long night in years gone by
And cried, "At last my question meets reply."

SONG

By AUBREY DE VERE

Seek not the tree of silkiest bark
  And balmiest bud,
To carve her name while yet 'tis dark
  Upon the wood!
The world is full of noble tasks
  And wreaths hard won:
Each work demands strong hearts, strong hands,
  Till day is done.

Sing not that violet-veined skin,
  That cheek's pale roses,
The lily of that form wherein
  Her soul reposes!
Forth to the fight, true man! true knight!
  The clash of arms
Shall more prevail than whisper'd tale,
  To win her charms.

The Warrior for the True, the Right,
  Fights in Love's name;

The love that lures thee from that flight
  Lures thee to shame:
That love which lifts the heart, yet leaves
  The spirit free—
That love, or none, is fit for one
  Man-shap'd like thee.

THE SONS OF PATRICK

By JAMES B. DOLLARD

Into the mists of the Pagan island
  Bearing God's message great Patrick came;
The Druid altars on plain and highland
  Fell at the sound of his mighty name!

Swift was the conquest—with hearts upswelling
  The Faith they took, and to God they swore:
That precious spark from their bosoms' dwelling,
  Man's guile or torture should snatch no more.

And ever since, while the wide world wonders
  This steadfast people their strength reveal,
As Time Earth's kingdoms and empires sunders,
  They stand by Patrick in ranks of steel!

The nations mock them, like Christ's tormentors;
  "Descend," they cry, "from your cross of shame;
Abjure the Faith—see the road that enters
  The groves of pleasure and wealth and fame!"

Like those that passed where the Cross rose dimly
  Their wise beards wagging—"What fools!" they say;
But the Sons of Patrick make answer grimly:
  "Our God we've chosen—the price we'll pay.

"Ever about us the foes' commotion,
  The anguish sweat on our brows ne'er dry;
Our martyr's bones strew the land and ocean,
  Lone deserts echo our exiles' cry.

"Unto our hearts is earth's pride forbidden,
  Unto our hands is its gold denied;
We do not question the Purpose hidden—
  Let Him who fashioned our souls decide!

"Yet though once more to us choice were given,
  And the long aeons were backward rolled,
We'd walk again before Earth and Heaven
  The blood-stained pathway we walked of old!"

SONG OF THE LITTLE VILLAGES

By JAMES B. DOLLARD

The pleasant little villages that grace the Irish glynns
Down among the wheatfields—up amid the whins,
The little white-walled villages crowding close together,
Clinging to the Old Sod in spite of wind and weather:
  Ballytarsney, Ballymore, Ballyboden, Boyle,
  Ballingarry, Ballymagorry by the Banks of Foyle,
  Ballylaneen, Ballyporeen, Bansha, Ballysadare,
  Ballybrack, Ballinalack, Barna, Ballyclare.

The cozy little villages that shelter from the mist,
Where the great West Walls by ocean spray are kissed;
The happy little villages that cuddle in the sun
When blackberries ripen and the harvest work is done.
  Corrymeela, Croaghnakeela, Clogher, Cahirciveen,
  Cappaharoe, Carrigaloe, Cashel and Coosheen,
  Castlefinn, Carrigtohill, Crumlin, Clara, Clane,
  Carrigaholt, Carrigaline, Cloghjordan and Coolrain.

The dreamy little villages, where by the fires at night,
Old Sanachies with ghostly tale the boldest hearts affright;
The crooning of the wind-blast is the wailing Banshee's cry,
And when the silver hazels stir they say the fairies sigh,
  Kilfenora, Kilfinnane, Kinnity, Killylea,
  Kilmoganny, Kiltamagh, Kilronan and Kilrea,

Killashandra, Kilmacow, Killiney, Killashee,
Killenaule, Killmyshall, Killorglin and Killeagh.

Leave the little villages, o'er the black sea go,
Learn the stranger's welcome, learn the exile's woe,
Leave the little villages, but think not to forget,
Afar they'll rise before your eyes to rack your bosoms yet.
Moneymore, Moneygall, Monivea and Moyne,
Mullinahone, Mullinavatt, Mullagh and Mooncoin,
Shanagolden, Shanballymore, Stranorlar and Slane,
Toberaheena, Toomyvara, Tempo and Strabane.

On the Southern Llanos—north where strange light gleams,
Many a yearning exile sees them in his dreams;
Dying voices murmur (passed all pain and care),
"Lo, the little villages, God has heard our prayer."
Lisdoonvarna, Lissadil, Lisdargan, Lisnaskea,
Portglenone, Portarlington, Portumna, Portmagee,
Clondalkin and Clongowan, Cloondara and Clonae,
God bless the little villages and guard them night and day!

THE SOUL OF KARNAGHAN BUIDHE

By James B. Dollard

It was the soul of Karnaghan Buidhe
Left his lips with a groan.

Like arrowy lightning bolt released
　　It sprang to the Judgment throne.

Spoke the Judge: "For as many years
　　As the numbered drops of the sea
I grant you heaven—but thenceforth hell,
　　Your bitter lot shall be."

Prayed the soul of Karnaghan Buidhe
　　(*The trembling soul of Karnaghan Buidhe*)
"Dear Lord, who died on Calvary,
　　Too brief that span of heaven for me."

Then spoke the Lord: "For as many years
　　As numbered sands on the shore,
The joys of heaven I give—but thence
　　You'll see my face no more."

Pleaded the soul of Karnaghan Buidhe
　　(*The shuddering soul of Karnaghan Buidhe*)
"Blessed Lord who died on the shameful tree,
　　Too brief that span of heaven for me."

Once more the Judge: "The blades of grass
　　That earth-winds ever blew
A year of heaven I'll count for each
　　Till hell shall yawn for you."

Prayed the soul of Karnaghan Buidhe
(*The anguished soul of Karnaghan Buidhe*)
"Kind Lord, who died in agony,
Too brief that spell of heaven for me.

But this I ask, O Christ—a year
Of hell for each of these:
The blades of grass, the grains of sand,
The drops that make the seas!
And after this, sweet Lord, with Thee
In heaven for all eternity!"

Spoke the Judge, and His smile of love
Gladdened the waiting choir above:
"Sin and sorrow forever past,
Heaven I grant you, first and last!"

THE ANGELIC CHORUS

By D. J. DONAHOE

At midnight from the zenith burst a light
More radiant and more beautiful than dawn,
And the meek shepherds on the shadowy lawn
Gazed upward in mute wonder on the sight;
The stars sank back in pallor, and the skies
Trembled responsive to rich harmonies.

And lo! an angel spake, "Be not afraid!
  I bear glad tidings; for this happy morn
  A Saviour and a King to man is born;
He sleepeth in a manger lowly laid."
Then rolled along the heavens the glad refrain;
"Glory to God on high and peace to men!"

Soon from the skies the streaming light was gone,
   And Night and Silence rested on the hill;
   But the mute shepherds, looking upward still,
Could hear the heavenly echoes rolling on.
So evermore the listening world can hear
The Angelic Chorus ringing sweet and clear.

LADYE CHAPEL AT EDEN HALL

By Eleanor C. Donnelly

Close to the Sacred Heart, it nestles fair—
A marble poem; an aesthetic dream
Of sculptured beauty, fit to be the theme
Of angel fancies; a Madonna-prayer
Uttered in stone. Round columns light as air,
And fretted cornice, Sharon's Rose is wreathed—
The passion-flower, the thorn-girt lily rare,
The palm, the wheat, the grapes in vine-leaves sheathed.
Tenderly bright, from mullioned windows glow

Our Lady's chaplet-mysteries. Behold,
Her maiden statue in that shrine of snow,
Looks upward to the skies of blue and gold;
Content that in the crypt, beneath her shining feet,
The holy ones repose in dreamless slumber sweet.

MARY IMMACULATE

By ELEANOR C. DONNELLY

"Pure as the snow," we say. Ah! never flake
    Fell through the air
    One-tenth as fair
As Mary's soul was made for Christ's dear sake.
    Virgin Immaculate,
The whitest whiteness of the Alpine snows,
Beside thy stainless spirit, dusky grows.
"Pure as the stars." Ah! never lovely night
    Wore in its diadem
    So pure a gem
As that which fills the ages with its light.
    Virgin Immaculate,
The peerless splendors of thy soul by far
Outshine the glow of heaven's serenest star.

THE PILGRIM

By ELEANOR DOWNING

Behind me lies the mistress of the East,
  Golden in evening, fairy dome on dome
  Poised and irised like the far-flung foam
  Lashed on the ribs of some forsaken coast.
  Wicked and lovely temptress, fruitless boast
Of all that man may build and little be,
Mart of the world's base passions, where thy feast
Of shame was spread, thy sin encompassed me,
  Where all desires and all dreams were rife
  With lust of flesh and eye and pride of life,
  Lo! I have reft thy carnal mastery—
  I have gone forth and shut the gates of thee.

Before me lies the desert and the night,
  White star and gold above a pathless waste,
  Blue shade and gray to where the world effaced
  Flings loose its shadows on the lap of God.
  Briars and dust upon my brow, unshod,
In pilgrim weeds athwart a vineless land,
My feet shall pass and mark the path aright,
For lo! Thy staff and rod are in my hand;
  And with the light Thy city shall unfurl
  Its golden oriflames and tents of pearl—
  Dead Babylon, thy gilden clasp I flee;
  Jerusalem, lift up thy gates to me!

ON THE FEAST OF THE ASSUMPTION

By ELEANOR DOWNING

"Mary, uplifted to our sight
In cloudy vesture stainless-white,
Why are thine eyes like stars alight,
　Twin flames of charity?"
"Mine eyes are on His glorious face
That shone not on earth's darkened place,
But clothed and crowned me with grace—
　The God who fathered me!"
"Mary, against the sinless glow
Of angel pinions white as snow,
Why are thy fair lips parted so
　In ecstasy of love?"
"My lips are parted to His breath
Who breathed on me in Nazareth
And gave me life to live in death—
　My Spouse, the spotless Dove!"
"Mary, whose eager feet would spurn
The very clouds, whose pale hands yearn
Toward rifted Heaven that fires burn
　Where once was fixed the sword?"
"The fires I felt when His child head
Lay on this mother's heart that bled,
And when it lay there stark and dead—
　My little Child, my Lord!"

MARY

By Eleanor Downing

A garden like a chalice-cup,
  With bloom of almond white and pink,
  And starred hibiscus to the brink,
From which sweet waters bubble up.
A garden walled with ilex-trees
  And topped with blue, white clouds between
  Save where the glossed leaves' twinkling green
Is stirred by some soft-footed breeze
A place apart, a watered glade,
  Where sin and sorrow have not been,
  And earth's complaint grows hushed within
Its greening aisles of sacred shade.

The circling arms, the flower face,
  Such were they to the Child soft-pressed,
  Who drew all sweetness from the breast
Of her whom angels crowned with grace.

A night of storm and wailing stress,
  A coast that cradles to the shock
  Of waves that lap the pitted rock,
And winds that shriek their wrathfulness;
A night of all wild things unpent,
  Strange voices and strange shapes that beat
  To chill the heart and snare the feet.

And through the tempest, beacon-bent
To shelter from the driving damp
  Bespeaking warmth and sweet repose
  Within its sanctuary close,
The welcome of a red shrine-lamp.

So unto Him Who, weary, pressed
  Through the fierce storm of wrath and hate,
  Shone Mary's love, a chapel-gate
Where He might enter Him and rest.

A desert filled with shining sand,
  And still as death the skies that bend
  Where to horizon without end
The rounding distances expand.
A desert white with burning heat
  And parched silence without stir,
  And at its heart a voyager,
Where Death and daggered noonday meet;
And Thirst that grips him by the throat;
  When from the distance wreathing blue,
  No mirage, but a dream come true,
Crowned palm-tree and pale waters float.

To Christ upon the rood, when dim
  Fell on His brow the Shade accurst,
  So Mary slaked His burning thirst
With her white soul held up to Him.

EXTREME UNCTION

By ERNEST DOWSON

Upon the eyes, the lips, the feet,
  On all the passages of sense,
The atoning oil is spread with sweet
  Renewal of lost innocence.

The feet, that lately ran so fast
  To meet desire, are soothly sealed;
The eyes, that were so often cast
  On vanity, are touched and healed.

From troublous sights and sounds set free
  In such a twilight hour of breath,
Shall one retrace his life, or see,
  Through shadows, the true face of death?

Vials of mercy! Sacring oils!
  I know not where nor when I come,
Nor through what wanderings and toils,
  To crave of you Viaticum.

Yet, when the walls of flesh grow weak,
  In such an hour, it well may be,
Through mist and darkness, light will break,
  And each anointed sense will see.

BENEDICTIO DOMINI

By ERNEST DOWSON

Without, the sullen noises of the street!
The voice of London, inarticulate,
Hoarse and blaspheming, surges in to meet
The silent blessing of the Immaculate.

Dark is the church, and dim the worshippers,
    Hushed with bowed heads as though by some old spell,
While through the incense-laden air there stirs
    The admonition of a silver bell.

Dark is the church, save where the altar stands,
    Dressed like a bride, illustrious with light,
Where one old priest exalts with tremulous hands
    The one true solace of man's fallen plight.

Strange silence here: without, the sounding street
    Heralds the world's swift passage to the fire;
O Benediction, perfect and complete!
    When shall men cease to suffer and desire?

CARTHUSIANS

By ERNEST DOWSON

Through what long heaviness, assayed in what strange fire,
   Have these white monks been brought into the way
      of peace,
Despising the world's wisdom and the world's desire,
   Which from the body of this death bring no release?

Within their austere walls no voices penetrate;
   A sacred silence only, as of death, obtains;
Nothing finds entry here of loud or passionate;
   This quiet is the exceeding profit of their pain.

From many lands they came, in divers fiery ways;
   Each knew at last the vanity of earthly joys;
And one was crowned with thorns, and one was crowned
      with bays,
   And each was tired at last of the world's foolish noise.

It was not theirs with Dominic to preach God's holy wrath,
   They were too stern to bear sweet Francis' gentle sway;
Theirs was a higher calling and a steeper path,
   To dwell alone with Christ, to meditate and pray.

A cloistered company, they are companionless,
   None knoweth here the secret of his brother's heart:

They are but come together for more loneliness,
Whose bond is solitude and silence all their part.

O beatific life! Who is there shall gainsay,
Your great refusal's victory, your little loss,
Deserting vanity for the more perfect way,
The sweetest service of the most dolorous Cross.

Ye shall prevail at last! Surely ye shall prevail!
Your silence and your austerity shall win at last:
Desire and Mirth, the world's ephemeral lights shall fail,
The sweet star of your queen is never overcast.

We fling up flowers and laugh, we laugh across the wine;
With wine we dull our souls and careful strains of art;
Our cups are polished skulls round which the roses twine:
None dares to look at Death who leers and lurks apart.

Move on, white company, whom that has not sufficed!
Our viols cease, our wine is death, our roses fail:
Pray for our heedlessness, O dwellers with the Christ!
Though the world fall apart, surely ye shall prevail.

MARIS STELLA

By AUGUSTA THEODOSIA DRANE

Mary, beautiful and bright
    "Velut Maris Stella,"
Brighter than the morning light,
    "Parens et Puella,"
I cry to thee, look down on me;
Ladye, pray thy Son for me,
    "Tam pia,"
That thy child may come to thee,
    "Maria."

Sad the earth was and forlorn,
    "Eva peccatrice,"
Until Christ our Lord was born
    "De te Genitrice";
Gabriel's "Ave" chased away
Darksome night, and brought the day
    "Salutis";
Thou the Fount whence waters play
    "Virtutis."

Ladye, Flower of living thing,
    "Rosa sine spina";
Mother of Jesus, heaven's King,
    "Gratia divinia";
'Tis thou in all dost bear the prize,

Ladye, Queen of Paradise,
    "Electa,"

Maiden meek and Mother wise,
    "Effecta."
In care thou counsellest the best,
    "Felix fecundata";
To the weary thou are rest,
    "Mater honorata";
Plead in thy love to Him who gave
His precious Blood the world to save
    "In cruce,"
That we our home with Him may have
    "In luce."

Well knows he, that he is thy Son,
    "Ventre quem portasti";
All thou dost ask Him, then, is won,
    "Partum quem lactasti";
So pitiful He is and kind,
By Him the road to bliss we find
    "Superni";
He doth the gates of darkness bind
    "Inferni."

AN AUTUMN ROSE-TREE

By MICHAEL EARLS, S.J.

It seemed too late for roses
  When I walked abroad today,
October stood in silence,
  By the hedges all the way:
Yet did I hear a singing,
  And I saw a red rose-tree:
In fields so gray with autumn
  How could song or roses be?

Oh, it was never maple
  Nor the dogwood's coat afire,
No sage with scarlet banners,
  Nor the poppy's vested choir:
The breeze that may be music
  When the summer lawns are fair
Will have no heart for singing
  In the autumn's mournful air.

As I went up the roadway,
  Under cold and lonely skies,
A song I heard, a rose-tree
  Waved to me in glad surprise:
A red cloak and a ribbon,
  (Round the braided hair of jet)

And redder cheeks than roses
  Of a little Margaret.

Now God is good in autumn,
  He can name the birds that sing,
He loves the hearts of children
  More than flowery fields of spring:
And when the years of winter
  Gray with Margaret will be,
God will find her love still blossom
  Like a red rose-tree.

TO A CARMELITE POSTULANT
(SAN FRANCISCO, MAY, 1910)

By MICHAEL EARLS, S.J.

Oh, the banks of May are fair,
  Charm of sound and sight,
Breath of heaven fills the air,
  To the world's delight.
Far more wondrous is a bower,
  Fairer than the May,
Love-of-God it wears in flower,
  Blooming night and day.
Love-of-God within the heart
  Multicolored grows,

Now a lily's counterpart,
  Now the blood-red rose.
Come the sun or chilling rain,
  Come the drought or dew,
Crocus health or violet pain,
  Love-of-God is true.
Hard may be the mountain-side,
  Soft the valley sod,
Yet will fragrance sure abide
  With the Love-of-God.
Where the grace of Heaven leads,
  There it makes a home,
Hills a hundred and the meads
  Will its pathway roam.
Carmel by the western sea
  Holds your blessed bower:
Love-of-God eternally
  Keep your heart a-flower.

A PURPOSE OF AMENDMENT

By HELEN PARRY EDEN

He who mangold-patch doth hoe,
Sweating beneath a sturdy sun,
Clearing each weed-disguised row
Till day-light and the task be done,

Standeth to view his labour's scene—
Where now, within the hedge-row's girth,
The little plants untrammeled green
Stripes the brown fabric of the earth.

So when the absolution's said
Behind the grille, and I may go,
And all the flowers of sin are dead,
And all the stems of sin laid low,

And I am come to Mary's shrine
To lay my hopes within her hand—
Ah, in how fair and green a line
The seedling resolutions stand.

THE CONFESSIONAL

By HELEN PARRY EDEN

My Sorrow diligent would sweep
That dingy room infest
With dust (thereby I mean my soul)
Because she hath a Guest
Who doth require that self-same room
Be garnished for His rest.

And Sorrow (who had washed His feet
Where He before had been)

Took the long broom of Memory
And swept the corners clean,
Till in the midst of the fair floor
The sum of dust was seen.

It lay there, settled by her tears,
That fell the while she swept—
Light fluffs of grey and earthly dregs;
And over these she wept,
For all were come since last her Guest
Within the room had slept.

And, for nor broom nor tears had power
To lift the clods of ill,
She called one servant of her Guest
Who came with right good will,
For, by his sweet Lord's bidding, he
Waiteth on Sorrow still;

So, seeing she had done her part
As far as in her lay
And had intent to keep the place
More cleanly from that day,
Did with his Master's dust-pan come
And take the dust away.

She thanked him, and Him who sent
Such succor, and she spread
Fair sheets of Thankfulness and Love

Upon her Master's bed,
Then on the new-scoured threshold stood
And listened for His tread.

AN ELEGY

FOR FATHER ANSELM, OF THE ORDER OF REFORMED CISTERCIANS, GUEST-MASTER AND PARISH PRIEST

"Et pastores erant in regione eadem vigilantes."

By HELEN PARRY EDEN

You to whose soul a death propitious brings
Its Heaven, who attain a windless bourne
Of sanctity beyond all sufferings,
It is not ours to mourn;

For you, to whom the earth could nothing give,
Who knew no hint of our inspired pride,
You could not very well be said to live
Until the day you died.

'Tis upon us—father and kindly friend,
Holy and cheerful host—the unbidden guest
You welcomed and the souls you would amend,
The weight of sorrow rests.

From Sarum in the mesh of her five streams,
Her idle belfries and her glittering vanes,
We are clomb to where the cloud-race dusks and gleams
On turf of upland plains.

Southward the road through juniper and briar
Clambers the down, untrodden and unworn
Save where some flock pitted the chalky mire
With little feet at dawn.

Twice in a week the hooded carrier's lamp,
Flashing on wayside flints and grasses, spills
Its misty radiance where the dews lie damp
Among the untended hills;

Here lies the hamlet ringed with grassy mound
And brambled barrow where, superbly dead,
The dust of pagans turned to holy ground
Beneath your humble tread.

Here we descend at drooping dusk the side
Of the stony down beneath the planted ring
Of beeches where you showed with pastoral pride
The folded lambs in spring;

Here pull at eve the self-same bell that hastened
Your rough-shod feet behind the hollow door—
Yet never see you stand, the chain unfastened,
Your lantern on the floor.

Others will spread the board now you are gone
Here where you smiled and gave your guests to eat,
Learning your menial kingliness from One
Who washed His servant's feet;

Along the slumbering corridors betimes
Others will knock and other footsteps pass
Down the wet lane e'er the thin shivering chimes
Toll for the early mass.

Yet in the chapel's self no sorrows sing
In the strange priest's voice, nor any dolour grips
The heart because it is not you who bring
Your Master to its lips.

Here let us leave the things you would not have—
Vain grief and sorrow useless to be shown—
"God's gift and the Community's I gave
And nothing of my own,"

You would have said, self-deemed of no more worth
That then green hands that guard a poppy's grace—
Blows the eternal flower and back to earth
Tumbles the withered case.

Nay, but Our Lord hath made renouncement vain,
Himself into those humble hands let fall,
Guerdon of willing poverty and pain,
The greatest gift of all;

To you and all who in that life austere
Mid fields remote your harsher labours ply
Singing His praise, girt round from year to year
With sheep-bells and the sky—

This, that to you is larger audience given
Where prayer and praise with sighing pinions shod
Piercing the starry ante-rooms of Heaven
Sway the designs of God:

And now yourself, standing where late hath stood
The echo of your voice, are prayer and praise—
O sweet reward and unsurpassing good
For that small gift of days.

Yourself, who now have heard such summoning
And seen such burning clarities alight
As broke the vigilant shepherds' drowsy ring
On the predestined night,

Who made such haste as theirs who rose and trod
To Bethlehem the dew-encumbered grass,
Trustful to see the showing forth of God
And the Word come to pass;

With how much more than home-spun Israelites'
Poor hungry glimpse of Godhead are you blest
Whom Mary shows for more than mortal nights
The Jewel on her breast.

Yet, as one kneeling churl might chance to think
Of the wan herd behind their wattled bars,
Moving unshepherded with bells that clink
And stir beneath the stars,

And, for the thought's space wishing he were back,
Pray, to that Sum of Sweetness for his sheep—
"Take them, O Thou that dost supply our lack,
Into Thy hands to keep."

So you who in His presence move and live
Recall amid your glad celestial cares,
Your chosen office, to your children give
The charity of prayers.

SORROW

By HELEN PARRY EDEN

Of Sorrow, 'tis as Saints have said—
That his ill-savoured lamp shall shed
A light to Heaven, when, blown about
By the world's vain and windy rout,
The candles of delight burn out.

Then usher Sorrow to thy board,
Give him such fare as may afford

Thy single habitation—best
To meet him half-way in his quest,
The importunate and sad-eyed guest.

Yet somewhat should he give who took
My hospitality, for look,
His is no random vagrancy;
Beneath his rags what hints there be
Of a celestial livery.

Sweet Sorrow, play a grateful part,
Break me the marble of my heart
And of its fragments pave a street
Where, to my bliss, myself may meet
One hastening with piercèd feet.

OUR LADY'S DEATH

By FATHER EDMUND, C.P.

And didst thou die, dear Mother of our Life?
    Sin had no part in thee; then how should death?
    Methinks, if aught the great tradition saith
Could wake in loving hearts a moment's strife
(I said—my own with her new image rife),

'Twere this. And yet 'tis certain, next to faith
    Thou didst lie down to render up thy breath:
    Though after the seventh sword, no meaner knife

Could pierce that bosom. No, nor did: no sting
    Of pain was there; but only joy. The love,
    So long thy life ecstatic, and restrained
From setting free thy soul, now gave it wing;
    Thy body, soon to reign with it above,
    Radiant and fragrant, as in trance, remained.

VIGIL OF THE IMMACULATE CONCEPTION

By MAURICE FRANCIS EGAN

A sword of silver cuts the fields asunder—
    A silver sword tonight, a lake in June—
And plains of snow reflect, the maples under,
    The silver arrows of a wintry noon.

The trees are white with moonlight and with ice-pearls;
    The trees are white, like ghosts we see in dreams;
The air is still: there are no moaning wind-whirls;
    And one sees silence in the quivering beams.

December night, December night, how warming
    Is all thy coldness to the Christian soul:

Thy very peace at each true heart is storming
  In potent waves of love that surging roll.

December night, December night, how glowing
  Thy frozen rains upon our warm hearts lie:
Our God upon this vigil is bestowing
  A thousand graces from the silver sky.

O moon, O symbol of our Lady's whiteness;
  O snow, O symbol of our Lady's heart;
O night, chaste night, bejewelled with argent brightness,
  How sweet, how bright, how loving, kind thou art.

O miracle: tomorrow and tomorrow,
  In tender reverence shall no praise abate;
For from all seasons shall we new jewels borrow
  To deck the Mother born Immaculate.

THE OLD VIOLIN

By MAURICE FRANCIS EGAN

Though tuneless, stringless, it lies there in dust,
  Like some great thought on a forgotten page;
The soul of music cannot fade or rust—
  The voice within it stronger grows with age;

Its strings and bow are only triffling things—
A master-touch!—its sweet soul wakes and sings.

MAURICE DE GUERIN

By MAURICE FRANCIS EGAN

The old wine filled him, and he saw, with eyes
   Anoint of Nature, fauns and dryads fair
   Unseen by others; to him maidenhair
And waxen lilacs, and those birds that rise
A-sudden from tall reeds at slight surprise,
   Brought charmed thoughts; and in earth everywhere
   He, like sad Jaques, found a music rare
As that of Syrinx to old Grecians wise.
A pagan heart, a Christian soul had he,
   He followed Christ, yet for dead Pan he sighed,
   Till earth and heaven met within his breast;
As if Theocritus in Sicily
   Had come upon the Figure crucified
   And lost his gods in deep, Christ-given rest.

HE MADE US FREE

By Maurice Francis Egan

As flame streams upward, so my longing thought
    Flies up with Thee,
Thou God and Saviour who hast truly wrought
Life out of death, and to us, loving, brought
A fresh, new world; and in Thy sweet chains caught,
    And made us free!

As hyacinths make way from out the dark,
    My soul awakes,
At thought of Thee, like sap beneath the bark;
As little violets in field and park
Rise to the trilling thrush and meadow-lark,
    New hope it takes.

As thou goest upward through the nameless space
    We call the sky,
Like jonquil perfume softly falls Thy grace;
It seems to touch and brighten every place;
Fresh flowers crown our wan and weary race,
    O Thou on high.

Hadst Thou not risen, there would be no more joy
    Upon earth's sod;
Life would still be with us a wound or toy,
A cloud without the sun—O Babe, O Boy,

A Man of Mother pure, with no alloy,
    O risen God!

Thou, God and King, didst "mingle in the game,"
    (Cease, all fears; cease!)
For love of us—not to give Virgil's fame
Or Croesus' wealth, not to make well the lame,
Or save the sinner from deserved shame,
    But for sweet Peace!

For peace, for joy—not that the slave might lie
    In luxury,
Not that all woe from us should always fly,
Or golden crops with Syrian roses vie
In every field; but in Thy peace to die
    And rise—be free!

THE GRANDEURS OF MARY

By FREDERICK WILLIAM FABER, D.D.

What is this grandeur I see up in heaven,
  A splendour that looks like a splendour divine?
What creature so near the Creator is throned?
  O Mary, those marvellous glories are thine.
But who would have thought that a creature could live
  With the fires of the Godhead so awfully nigh?

Oh, who could have dreamed, mighty Mother of God,
    That ever God's power could have raised thee so high?

What name can we give to a queenship so grand?
    What thought can we think of a glory like this?
Saints and angels lie far in the distance, remote
    From the golden excess of thine unmated bliss.
Thy person, thy soul, thy most beautiful form,
    Thine office, thy name, thy most singular grace—
God hath made for them, Mother, a world by itself,
    A shrine all alone, a most worshipful place.

Mid the blaze of those fires, eternal, unmade,
    Thy Maker unspeakably makes thee his own;
The arms of the Three Uncreated, outstretched,
    Round the Word's mortal Mother in rapture are thrown.
Thy sinless conception, thy jubilant birth,
    Thy crib and thy cross, thine assumption and crown,
They have raised thee on high to the right hand of Him
    Whom the spells of thy love to thy bosom drew down.

I am blind with thy glory; in all God's wide world
    I find nothing like thee for glory and power:
I can hardly believe that thou grewest on earth,
    In the green fields of Juda, a scarce-noticed flower.
And is it not really eternal, divine?
    Is it human, created, a glorified heart,
So like God, and not God? Ah, Maker of men,
    We bless thee for being the God that thou art.

O Mary, what ravishing pageants I see,
　What wonders and works centre round thee in heaven,
What creations of grace fall like light from thy hands,
　What creator-like powers to thy prudence are given.
What vast jurisdiction, what numberless realms,
　What profusion of dread and unlimited power,
What holy supremacies, awful domains,
　The Word's mighty Mother enjoys for her dower.

What grand ministrations of pity and strength,
　What endless processions of beautiful light,
What incredible marvels of motherly love,
　What queenly resplendence of empire and right.
What sounds as of seas flowing all round thy throne,
　What flashings of fire from thy burning abode,
What thunders of glory, what tempests of power,
　What calms, like the calms in the Bosom of God.

Inexhaustible wonder; the treasures of God
　Seem to multiply under thy marvellous hand;
And the power of thy Son seems to gain and to grow,
　When He deigns to obey thy maternal command.
Ten thousand magnificent greatnesses blend
　Their vast oceans of light, at the foot of thy throne;
Ten thousand unspeakable majesties grace
　The royalty vested in Mary alone.

But look, what a wonder there is up in God:
　One love, like a special perfection, we see;

And the chief of thy grandeurs, great Mother, is there—
In the love the Eternal Himself has for thee.

THE RIGHT MUST WIN

By FREDERICK WILLIAM FABER, D.D.

Oh, it is hard to work for God,
  To rise and take His part
Upon this battlefield of earth,
  And not sometimes lose heart.
He hides Himself so wondrously,
  As though there were no God;
He is least seen when all the powers
  Of ill are most abroad.
Or He deserts us at the hour
  The fight is all but lost;
And seems to leave us to ourselves
  Just when we need Him most.
Ill masters good; good seems to change
  To ill with greatest ease;
And, worst of all, the good with good
  Is at cross-purposes.
Ah! God is other than we think;
  His ways are far above,
Far beyond reason's height, and reached
  Only by child-like love.

Workman of God! Oh, lose not heart,
  But learn what God is like;
And in the darkest battle-field
  Thou shalt know where to strike.
Thrice blessed is he to whom is given
  The instinct that can tell
That God is on the field when He
  Is most invisible.
Blessed too, is he who can divine
  Where real right doth lie,
And dares to take the side that seems
  Wrong to man's blindfold eye.
For right is right, since God is God;
  And right the day must win;
To doubt would be disloyalty,
  To falter would be sin.

MATER DOLOROSA

By JOHN FITZPATRICK, O.M.I.

She stands, within the shadow, at the foot
  Of the high tree she planted: thirty-three
  Full years have sped, and such has grown to be
The stem that burgeoned forth from Jesse's root.
Spring swiftly passed and panted in pursuit
  The eager summer; now she stands to see

The only fruit-time of her only tree:
And all the world is waiting for the Fruit.

Now is faith's sad fruition: this one hour
  Of gathered expectation wears the crown
    Of the long grief with which the years were rife;
As in her lap—a sudden autumn shower—
  The earthquake with his trembling hand shakes down
    The red, ripe Fruitage of the Tree of Life.

YULETIDE

By ALICE FURLONG

In a stable bare,
Lo, the great Ones are.
Strew the Ivy and the Myrtle
Round about the Virgin's kirtle!
Ass and oxen mild
Breathe soft upon the Child!
Blow the scent of bygone summer
On your breath to the New-comer!

Be ye well content
To be straitly pent
Backwards in the rocky chamber
From the angel's wings of amber!

Rapt the seraphs sit,
With godly faces lit
In a radiance shining solely
From the Christ-child, meek and holy.

High they chant and clear
Of the lovely cheer
Ring down the new evangels
Of the mystic, midnight angels.
Faring with good will
From the misty hill,
Every shepherd sacrificeth
To the prophet that ariseth.

Joseph, Mary's spouse,
Prince of David's House,
Bendeth low in adorations
To the Ruler of the Nations.
Who doth sweetly rest
On his Mother's breast,
Lord of the lightnings and the thunders!
Mary's heart keeps all these wonders.

OUR LADY OF THE ROSARY

By FRANCIS A. GAFFNEY, O.P.

Lepanto marks the spot of victory,
  O'er crescent cruel and strong, by forces weak,
  Of hallowed cross; of which, "if sign you seek,"
'Tis not of man but a Divinity.
The white-robed Pius Fifth the Rosary
  Uplifted like the rod of Moses, meek;
  Whilst Ottomans on Christians wrath would wreak
And, as of old, engulfed them in the sea.

O Lady of the Rosary today,
  Thy clients all beseech thee, hear their prayer,
    And beg the Christ Who raging storms did quell,
Bid warring nations cease their bloody fray;
  His power and thine honor, we declare,
    O Thou All-Fair, thou joy of Israel.

AT THE LEAP OF THE WATERS

By EDWARD F. GARESCHÉ, S.J.

How the swift river runs bright to its doom,
  Placid and shining and smooth-flowing by,
Blue with the gleam of the heavenly room,

Smiling and calm with the smile of the sky!
Ah, but the plunge! and the shock and the roar,
  The spray of vast waters that hurl to the deep,
The churn of its foam, as the measureless pour
  Of that wide-brimming torrent leaps sheer from the steep!
Look ye; it reaches small fingers of spray
  To clutch at the brink, as unwilling to go
Through the perilous air, and be fretted away
  In the tumult of vapor that boileth below.
List ye! the voice of the huge undertone
  That murmurs in pain from the cataract's breast,
Where the bruised, shattered waters perpetual moan
  And wander and toss in a weary unrest.
Feel ye the breath of the cool-spraying mist,
  Cloudy and gray from the depths of its pain;
Not as when sunbeams the waters have kissed,
  Rising in vapor to gather in rain,
But fiercely and madly flung forth on the air,
  A shroud for this river that leaps to its death,
A veil o'er the throes of the cataract there,
  And rolling and rent with its agonized breath!
Wild torrent! God put thee to thunder His name!
  With the roar of thy waters to call to the sky
Of His might, Who hath set thee forever the same,
  To topple in foam to the gulfs from on high.
Loud hymn of the lake-lands! from shore unto shore,
  Still clamor His praises Who called thee to be,
Till the ears of the nations are tuned to thy roar,
  And they hear the vast message He trusted to thee.

NIAGARA

By EDWARD F. GARESCHÉ, S.J.

God, in His ages past the dawn of days,
Writ one white line of praise,
Which now, in this great stress and hour of need,
I bend my soul to read.
I break the sullen bonds of wearying time,
And with one leap sublime,
Force my astounded soul go back and stand
In the primaeval land!

The tresses of the ancient flood are kissed
With virginal, white mist.
The same soft, thunderous sound
Thrills the wild woods around,
But oh the vast and mighty peace that broods
On these green solitudes,
Where the great land, with one tremendous tone,
Litanies to God, alone!

Tongue of the continent! Thou whose hymning shakes
The bosom of the lakes!
O sacrificial torrent, keen and bright,
Hurled from thy glorious height!
Thou sacerdotal presence, clothed in power,
At once the victim and the white-robed priest,
Whose praise throughout these ages hath not ceased,

Whose altar steams with incense every hour!
Lo, in all days, from thy white waters, rise
The savors of perpetual sacrifice!
I see pale prophecy of Christ's dear blood!—
The transubstantiation of thy flood!

Oh the wild wonder of the vast emotion
Of the perturbed wave,
That cries and wanders like the fearful ocean,
Seeking, with none to save!
In their wide agony the rapids roam,
A world of waves, an universe of pain!
The vexed, tumultous clamor of their foam
Crying to God with agonized refrain,
Where the sad rocks their quivering summits hide
In the loud anguish of the refluent tide.

Yet, with a willingness that leaps to sorrow
Swift run the ragged surges to the height,
And from their pain is born a pure delight—
The fear today, the snowy peace tomorrow!—
Cleaving like darts their swift and silvery way
With sudden gleams, and barbs of glittering spray,
They hurry to the brink, and swift are lost
In that stupendous leap, that infinite holocaust!

Oh Christ-like glory of the praying water
That leaps forever to its mystic death!
And from the anguish of that sobbing slaughter

Lifts the clear glory of the torrent's breath,
Where like a paean of rapturous victory calls
The solemn jubilation of the falls!

O alabastrine priest—thy splendor spraying
More lasting than the immemorial hills!
O monument of waves, O undecaying
While God's right hand thy flowing chalice fills!
Under the transient world's astonished eyes
Thou offerest abiding sacrifice!

In the pale morning, when the rising sun
Flatters thy pouring flood with slanting beams,
Most reverent thy duteous waters run,
And hymn to God with all their thousand streams.
And in the blazing majesty of noon,
Still lifts thy wave its sacrificial tune,
And spills, like jewels of some eastern story,
Its bright, impetuous avalanche of glory!

And in the stilly spaces of the night,
While heaven wonders with its wakeful stars,
Thou prayest still, beneath the solemn light,
In booming tones that reach to heaven's bars,
Keeping thy vigils, while the angelic moon
Walks on thy perilous verge with glorious shoon,
Chanting from foam and spray without encease
Thy yearning immemorial prayer for peace!

COMMUNION

By CAROLINE GILTINAN

Mother Mary, thee I see
Bringing Him, thy Babe, to me,
Thou dost say, with trusting smile:
"Hold Him, dear, a little while."
Mother Mary, pity me,
For He struggles to be free!
My heart, my arms—He finds defiled:
I am unworthy of thy Child.
Mary, Mother, charity!
Bring thy Baby back to me!

THE NIGHTINGALE

By GERALD GRIFFIN

As the mute nightingale in closest groves
  Lies hid at noon, but when day's piercing eye
  Is locked in night, with full heart beating high
Poureth her plain-song o'er the light she loves;
So, Virgin Ever-pure and Ever-blest,
  Moon of religion, from whose radiant face
  Reflected streams the light of heavenly grace
On broken hearts, by contrite thoughts oppressed:

So, Mary, they who justly feel the weight
  Of Heaven's offended Majesty, implore
    Thy reconciling aid with suppliant knee:
Of sinful man, O sinless Advocate,
  To thee they turn, nor Him they less adore;
    'Tis still His light they love, less dreadful seen in thee.

TRYSTE NOEL

By LOUISE IMOGEN GUINEY

The Ox he openeth wide the doore,
  And from the Snowe he calls her inne,
And he hath seen her smile therefore,
  Our Ladye without Sinne.
    Now soone from Sleep
    A Starre shall leap,
And sonne arrive both King and Hinde:
          Amen, Amen:
But O the place co'd I but finde!

The Ox hath hushed his voyce and bent
  Trewe eyes of Pitty ore the Mow,
And on his lovelie Neck, forspent,
  The Blessed layes her Browe.
    Around her feet,
    Full Warme and Sweete,

His bowerie Breath doth meeklie dwell:
Amen, Amen:
But sore am I with Vaine Travel!

The Ox is Host in Judah stall
And Host of more than onlie one,
For close she gathereth withal
Our Lorde her littel Sonne.
Glad Hinde and King
Their Gyfte may bring,
But wo'd tonight my Teares were there,
Amen, Amen:
Between her Bosom and His hayre!

THE WILD RIDE

By LOUISE IMOGEN GUINEY

I hear in my heart, I hear in its ominous pulses
All day, on the road, the hoofs of invisible horses,
All night, from their stalls, the importunate pawing
and neighing.

Let cowards and laggards fall back! but alert to the saddle,
Weatherworn and abreast, go men of our galloping legion,
With a stirrup-cup each to the lily of women that loves him.

The trail is through dolor and dread, over crags and morasses;
There are shapes by the way, there are things that appal or
   entice us:
What odds? We are Knights of the Grail, we are vowed to
   the riding.

Thought's self is a vanishing wing, and joy is a cobweb,
And friendship a flower in the dust, and glory a sunbeam:
Not here is our prize, nor, alas! after these our pursuing.

A dipping of plumes, a tear, a shake of the bridle,
A passing salute to this world and her pitiful beauty:
We hurry with never a word in the track of our fathers.

I hear in my heart, I hear in its ominous pulses
All day, on the road, the hoofs of invisible horses,
All night, from their stalls, the importunate pawing
   and neighing.

We spur to a land of no name, outracing the stormwind;
We leap to the infinite dark like the sparks from the anvil.
Thou leadest, O God! All's well with Thy troopers that follow.

ODE FOR A MASTER MARINER ASHORE

By LOUISE IMOGEN GUINEY

There in his room, whene'er the moon looks in,
And silvers now a shell, and now a fin,
And o'er his chart glides like an argosy,
Quiet and old sits he.
Danger! he hath grown homesick for thy smile.
Where hidest thou the while, heart's boast,
Strange face of beauty sought and lost,
Star-face that lured him out from boyhood's isle?
Blown clear from dull indoors, his dreams behold
Night-water smoke and sparkle as of old,
The taffrail lurch, the sheets triumphant toss
Their phosphor-flowers across.
Towards ocean's either rim the long-exiled
Wears on, till stunted cedars throw
A lace-like shadow over snow,
Or tropic fountains wash their agates wild.

Awhile, play up and down the briny spar
Odors of Surinam and Zanzibar,
Till blithely thence he ploughs, in visions new,
The Labradorian blue;
All homeless hurricanes about him break;
The purples of spent day he sees
From Samos to the Hebrides,
And drowned men dancing darkly in his wake.

Where the small deadly foam-caps, well descried,
Top, tier on tier, the hundred-mountained tide,
Away, and far away, his pride is borne,
Riding the noisy morn,
Plunges, and preens her wings, and laughs to know
The helm and tightening halyards still
Follow the urging of his will,
And scoff at sullen earth a league below.

Mischance hath barred him from his heirdom high,
And shackled him with many an inland tie,
And of his only wisdom made a jibe
Amid an alien tribe:
No wave abroad but moans his fallen state,
The trade-wind ranges now, the trade-wind roars!
Why is it on a yellowing page he pores?
Ah, why this hawser fast to a garden gate?

Thou friend so long withdrawn, so deaf, so dim,
Familiar Danger, O forget not him!
Repeat of thine evangel yet the whole
Unto his subject soul,
Who suffers no such palsy of her drouth,
Nor hath so tamely worn her chain,
But she may know that voice again,
And shake the reefs with answer of her mouth.

O give him back, before his passion fail,
The singing cordage and the hollow sail,

And level with those aged eyes let be
The bright unsteady sea;
And move like any film from off his brain
The pasture wall, the boughs that run
Their evening arches to the sun,
The hamlet spire across the sown champaign;

And on the shut space and the trivial hour,
Turn the great floods! and to thy spousal bower,
With rapt arrest and solemn loitering,
Him whom thou lovedst bring:
That he, thy faithful one, with praising lip,
Not having, at the last, less grace
Of thee than had his roving race,
Sum up his strength to perish with a ship.

IN LEINSTER

By LOUISE IMOGEN GUINEY

I try to knead and spin, but my life is low the while.
Oh, I long to be alone, and walk abroad a mile;
Yet if I walk alone, and think of naught at all,
Why from me that's young should the wild tears fall?

The shower-stricken earth, the earth-colored streams,
They breathe on me awake, and moan to me in dreams;

And yonder ivy fondling the broke castle-wall,
It pulls upon my heart till the wild tears fall.

The cabin-door looks down, a furze-lighted hill,
And far as Leighlin Cross the fields are green and still;
But once I hear the blackbird in Leighlin hedges call,
The foolishness is on me, and the wild tears fall!

AUNT MARY
A CHRISTMAS CHANT

By ROBERT STEPHEN HAWKER

Now, of all the trees by the king's highway,
    Which do you love the best?
O! the one that is green upon Christmas Day,
    The bush with the bleeding breast.
Now the holly with her drops of blood for me:
For that is our dear Aunt Mary's tree.

Its leaves are sweet with our Saviour's Name,
    'Tis a plant that loves the poor:
Summer and winter it shines the same
    Beside the cottage door.
O! the holly with her drops of blood for me:
For that is our kind Aunt Mary's tree.

'Tis a bush that the birds will never leave:
 They sing in it all day long;
But sweetest of all upon Christmas Eve
 Is to hear the robin's song.
'Tis the merriest sound upon earth or sea:
For it comes from our own Aunt Mary's tree.

So, of all that grows by the king's highway,
 I love that tree the best;
'Tis a bower for the birds upon Christmas Day,
 The bush of the bleeding breast.
O! the holly with her drops of blood for me:
For that is our sweet Aunt Mary's tree.

KING ARTHUR'S WAES-HAEL

By ROBERT STEPHEN HAWKER

Waes-hael for knight and dame;
 O merry be their dole;
Drink-hael! In Jesu's name
 We fill the tawny bowl;
But cover down the curving crest,
Mould of the Orient Lady's breast.

Waes-hael! yet lift no lid:
 Drain ye the reeds for wine.

Drink-hael! the milk was hid
　That soothed that Babe divine;
Hush'd, as this hollow channel flows,
He drew the balsam from the rose.

Waes-hael! thus glowed the breast
　Where a God yearned to cling;
Drink-hael! so Jesu pressed
　Life from its mystic spring;
Then hush and bend in reverend sign
And breathe the thrilling reeds for wine.

Waes-hael! in shadowy scene
　Lo! Christmas children we:
Drink-hael! behold we lean
　At a far Mother's knee;
To dream that thus her bosom smiled,
And learn the lip of Bethlehem's Child.

OLD NUNS

By JAMES M. HAYES

Our Lady smiles on youthful nuns,
　She loves them well.
Our Lady's smile like sunshine floods
　Each convent cell,

But fondest falls Our Lady's smile
  Where old nuns dwell;

Old nuns whose hearts are young with love
  For Mary's Son,
Old nuns whose prayers for faltering souls
  Have victory won,
Old nuns whose lives are beautiful
  With service done.

Their love a loveless world has saved
  From God's dread rod,
The paths where Sorrow walks with Sin
  Their feet have trod,
Their knees have worn the flags that pave
  The house of God.

Our Lady smiles on youthful nuns,
  She loves them well;
Our Lady's smile like sunshine floods
  Each convent cell;
But fondest falls Our Lady's smile
  Where old nuns dwell.

THE MOTHER OF THE ROSE

By JAMES M. HAYES

I kneel on Holy Thursday with the faithful worshipping
Where Christ is throned in splendor as the sacramental King.

I ever will remember it, that wondrous full-blown rose
Among the burning tapers on the altar of repose.

O blessed among roses all, to bloom in beauty there,
To give your heart unto your God and in His glory share.

. . . .

In quiet fields beyond the town, near where the river flows
There is a humble garden where a gentle rose-tree grows.

Tonight Our Lord remembers on the altar of repose
This rose-tree in the fields afar, the mother of the rose.

THE TRANSFIGURATION

By JAMES M. HAYES

He seeks the mountains where the olives grow,
  The Lord of Glory, veiled in humble guise;

His soul is shadowed with a coming woe,
  The grief of all the world is in His eyes:
His spirit struggles in the dark caress
  Of anguish, pain and utter loneliness.

He always loved the mountain tops, for there
  Away from earth, He treads the mystic ways,
And sees the vision of the Fairest Fair,
  As Heaven dawns upon His raptured gaze;
The loneliness, the pain, the grief depart;
  Surpassing gladness fills His Sacred Heart.

That day He stood upon the olive hill,
  And Peter, James and John in wonder saw
The burning glories of the God-head fill
  His soul with grandeur, and in holy awe
They fell upon the ground and cried for grace,
  Lest they should die beholding God's own Face.

As minor chords that sob from strings of gold
  The Master speaks in accents sweet and sad:
The vision past, the chosen three behold
  No one but Jesus and their souls are glad.
The awe, the splendor and the glory gone,
  How sweet the face of Christ to look upon!

BELOVED, IT IS MORN

By EMILY H. HICKEY

Beloved, it is morn!
    A redder berry on the thorn,
    A deeper yellow on the corn,
For this good day new-born.
    Pray, Sweet, for me
    That I may be
    Faithful to God and thee.

Beloved, it is day!
    And lovers work, as children play,
    With heart and brain untired alway:
Dear love, look up and pray.
    Pray, Sweet, for me
    That I may be
    Faithful to God and thee.

Beloved, it is night!
    Thy heart and mine are full of light,
    Thy spirit shineth clear and white,
God keep thee in His sight!
    Pray, Sweet, for me
    That I may be
    Faithful to God and thee.

A SEA STORY

By EMILY H. HICKEY

Silence. A while ago
  Shrieks went up piercingly;
But now is the ship gone down;
  Good ship, well manned, was she.
There's a raft that's a chance of life for one,
  This day upon the sea.

A chance for one of two;
  Young, strong, are he and he,
Just in the manhood prime,
  The comelier, verily,
For the wrestle with wind and weather and wave,
  In the life upon the sea.

One of them has a wife
  And little children three;
Two that can toddle and lisp,
  And a suckling on the knee:
Naked they'll go, and hunger sore,
  If he be lost at sea.

One has a dream of home,
  A dream that well may be:
He never has breathed it yet;
  She never has known it, she.

But some one will be sick at heart
   If he be lost at sea.

"Wife and kids at home!—
   Wife, kids, nor home has he!—
Give us a chance, Bill!" Then,
   "All right, Jem!" Quietly
A man gives up his life for a man,
   This day upon the sea.

THE STARLIGHT NIGHT

By GERARD HOPKINS, S.J.

Look at the stars! look, look up at the skies!
   O look at all the fire-folk sitting in the air!
   The bright boroughs, the quivering citadels there!
The dim woods quick with diamond wells; the elf-eyes!
The grey lawns cold where quaking gold-dew lies!
   Wind-beat white-beam; airy abeles all on flare!
   Flake-doves sent floating out at a farmyard scare!—
Ah well! it is a purchase and a prize.

Buy then! Bid then!—What?—Prayer, patience, alms, vows,—
Look, look! a May-mess, like on orchard boughs;
   Look! March-bloom, like on mealed-with-yellow
      sallows.—

These are indeed the barn: within-doors house
    The shocks. This piece-bright paling hides the Spouse
    Christ, and the mother of Christ and all his hallows.

THE HABIT OF PERFECTION

By GERARD HOPKINS, S.J.

Elected Silence, sing to me
And beat upon my whorled ear,
Pipe me to pastures still and be
The music that I care to hear.

Shape nothing, lips; be lovely-dumb:
It is the shut, the curfew sent
From there where all surrenders come
Which only make you eloquent.

Be shelled, eyes, with double dark
And find the uncreated light;
This ruck and reel which you remark
Coils, keeps, and teases simple sight.

Palate, the hutch of tasty lust,
Desire not to be rinsed with wine:
The can must be so sweet, the crust
So fresh that come in fasts divine!

Nostrils, your careless breath that spend
Upon the stir and keep of pride,
What relish shall the censers send
Along the sanctuary side!

O feel-of-primrose hands, O feet
That want the yield of plushy sward,
But you shall walk the golden street,
And you unhouse and house the Lord.

And, Poverty, be thou the bride
And now the marriage feast begun,
And lily-colored clothes provide
Your spouse not labored-at, nor spun.

SPRING

By GERARD HOPKINS, S.J.

Nothing is so beautiful as spring—
  When weeds, in wheels, shoot long and lovely and lush:
    Thrush's eggs look little low heavens, and thrush
Through the echoing timber does so rinse and wring
The ear, it strikes like lightnings to hear him sing;
  The glassy pear-tree leaves and blooms, they brush
  The descending blue; that blue is all in a rush
With richness; the racing lambs too have fair their fling.

What is all this juice and all this joy?
A strain of the earth's sweet being in the beginning
In Eden garden. Have, get, before it cloy,
Before it cloud, Christ, lord, and sour with shining,
Innocent mind and Mayday in girl and boy,
Most, O maid's child, thy choice and worthy the winning.

THE FRIAR OF GENOA

By SCHARMEL IRIS

In Genoa a friar walked;
Of every sacred tale he talked;
Alone he dwelt, in prayer he knelt;
   "Ave Maria, Ave Maria!"
From dawn till dusk he sang.

His bruised and blistered feet were bare;
His head burned in the sunlight's glare.
On stones he slept, and worked and wept,
   "Ave Maria, Ave Maria!"
In every blow or pang.

Out of his dole he clothed the poor,
And every hardship did endure;
He blessed the meek and nursed the weak

"Ave Maria, Ave Maria!"
With each succeeding day.

And begged for alms for those in need,
A kind word spoke with every deed,
With sinners dined and led the blind—
    "Ave Maria, Ave Maria!"
Until he passed away.

And is his work done? Ah, surprise!
Out of the tomb where low he lies
A perfume blows, as of a rose:
    "Ave Maria, Ave Maria!"
It sings in shade or sun.

And he who breathes it, him it feeds,
And stirs his heart to noble deeds;
And one has said, "He is not dead—
    "Ave Maria, Ave Maria!
"His life has just begun!"

THE DARK ANGEL

By LIONEL JOHNSON

Dark Angel, with thine aching lust
To rid the world of penitence:

Malicious Angel, who still dost
My soul such subtile violence!

Because of thee, no thought, no thing,
Abides for me undesecrate:
Dark Angel, ever on the wing,
Who never reachest me too late!

When music sounds, then changest thou
Its silvery to a sultry fire:
Nor will thine envious heart allow
Delight untortured by desire.

Through thee, the gracious Muses turn
To Furies, O mine Enemy!
And all the things of beauty burn
With flames of evil ecstasy.

Because of thee, the land of dreams
Becomes a gathering place of fears:
Until tormented slumber seems
One vehemence of useless tears.

When sunlight glows upon the flowers,
Or ripples down the dancing sea:
Thou, with thy troop of passionate powers,
Beleaguerest, bewilderest, me.

Within the breath of autumn woods,
Within the winter silences:
Thy venomous spirit stirs and broods,
O Master of impieties!

The ardour of red flame is thine,
And thine the steely soul of ice:
Thou poisonest the fair design
Of nature, with unfair device.

Apples of ashes, golden bright;
Waters of bitterness, how sweet!
O banquet of a foul delight,
Prepared by thee, dark Paraclete!

Thou art the whisper in the gloom,
The hinting tone, the haunting laugh:
Thou art the adorner of my tomb,
The minstrel of mine epitaph.

I fight thee, in the Holy Name!
Yet, what thou dost, is what God saith:
Tempter! should I escape thy flame,
Thou wilt have helped my soul from Death:
The second Death, that never dies,
That cannot die, when time is dead:
Live Death, wherein the lost soul cries,
Eternally uncomforted.

Dark Angel, with thine aching lust!
Of two defeats, of two despairs:
Less dread, a change to drifting dust,
Than thine eternity of cares.

Do what thou wilt, thou shalt not so,
Dark Angel! triumph over me:
Lonely, unto the Lone I go;
Divine, to the Divinity.

TE MARTYRUM CANDIDATUS

By LIONEL JOHNSON

Ah, see the fair chivalry come, the companions of Christ!
White Horsemen, who ride on white horses, the Knights
    of God!
They, for their Lord and their Lover who sacrificed
All, save the sweetness of treading, where He first trod!
These through the darkness of death, the dominion of night,
Swept, and they woke in white places at morning tide:
They saw with their eyes, and sang for joy of the sight,
They saw with their eyes the Eyes of the Crucified.
Now, whithersoever He goeth, with Him they go:
White Horsemen, who ride on white horses, oh fair to see!
They ride, where the Rivers of Paradise flash and flow,
White Horsemen, with Christ their Captain: forever He!

CHRISTMAS AND IRELAND

By LIONEL JOHNSON

The golden stars give warmthless fire,
  As weary Mary goes through night:
Her feet are torn by stone and briar;
  She hath no rest, no strength, no light:
O Mary, weary in the snow,
  Remember Ireland's woe!

O Joseph, sad for Mary's sake!
  Look on our earthly Mother too:
Let not the heart of Ireland break
  With agony the ages through:

For Mary's love, love also thou
  Ireland, and save her now!
Harsh were the folk, and bitter stern,
  At Bethlehem, that night of nights.

For you no cheering hearth shall burn:
  We have no room here, you no rights.
O Mary and Joseph; hath not she,
  Ireland, been even as ye?

The ancient David's royal house
  Was thine, Saint Joseph! wherefore she,

Mary, thine Ever Virgin Spouse,
To thine own city went with thee.

Behold! thy citizens disown
The heir of David's throne!
Nay, more! The very King of Kings
Was with you, coming to His own:

They thrust Him forth to lowliest things;
The poor, meek beasts of toil alone
Stood by, when came to piteous birth
The God of all the earth.

And she, our Mother Ireland, knows
Insult, and infamies of wrong:
Her innocent children clad with woes,
Her weakness trampled by the strong:

And still upon her Holy Land
Her pitiless foemen stand.
From Manger unto Cross and Crown
Went Christ: and Mother Mary passed

Through Seven Sorrows, and sat down
Upon the Angel Throne at last.
Thence, Mary! to thine own Child pray,
For Ireland's hope this day!

She wanders amid winter still,
　The dew of tears is on her face:
Her wounded heart takes yet its fill
　Of desolation and disgrace.

God still is God! And through God she
　Foreknows her joy to be.
The snows shall perish at the spring,
　The flowers pour fragrance round her feet:

Ah, Jesus! Mary! Joseph! bring
　This mercy from the Mercy Seat!
Send it, sweet King of Glory, born
　Humbly on Christmas Morn!

TO MY PATRONS

By LIONEL JOHNSON

Thy spear rent Christ, when dead for me He lay:
　My sin rends Christ, though never one save He
Perfectly loves me, comforts me. Then pray,
　Longinus Saint! the Crucified, for me.
Hard is the holy war, and hard the way:
　At rest with ancient victors would I be.
O faith's first glory from our England! pray,
　St. Alban! to the Lord of Hosts, for me.

Fain would I watch with thee, till morning gray,
   Beneath the stars austere: so might I see
Sunrise, and light, and joy, at last. Then pray,
   John Baptist Saint! unto the Christ, for me.
Remembering God's coronation day;
   Thorns for His crown; His throne, a Cross: to thee
Heaven's kingdom dearer was than earth's. Then pray
   Saint Louis! to the King of kings, for me.
Thy love loved all things: thy love knew no stay,
   But drew the very wild beasts round thy knee.
O lover of the least and lowest! pray,
   Saint Francis! to the Son of Man, for me.
Bishop of souls in servitude astray,
   Who didst for holy service set them free:
Use still thy discipline of love, and pray.
   Saint Charles! unto the world's High Priest, for me.

OUR LADY OF THE SNOWS
(UPON READING THE POEM OF THAT NAME
IN THE UNDERWOODS OF MR. STEVENSON)

By LIONEL JOHNSON

Far from the world, far from delight,
Distinguishing not day from night;
Vowed to one sacrifice of all
The happy things, that men befall;

Pleading one sacrifice, before
Whom sun and sea and wind adore;
Far from earth's comfort, far away,
We cry to God, we cry and pray
For men, who have the common day.
Dance, merry world! and sing: but we,
Hearing, remember Calvary:
Get gold, and thrive you! but the sun
Once paled; and the centurion
Said: *This dead man was God's own Son.*
Think you, we shrink from common toil,
Works of the mart, works of the soil;
That, prisoners of strong despair,
We breathe this melancholy air;
Forgetting the dear calls of race,
And bonds of house, and ties of place;
That, cowards, from the field we turn,
And heavenward, in our weakness, yearn?
Unjust! unjust! while you despise
Our lonely years, our mournful cries:
You are the happier for our prayer;
The guerdon of our souls, you share.
Not in such feebleness of heart,
We play our solitary part;
Not fugitives of battle, we
Hide from the world, and let things be:
But rather, looking over earth,
Between the bounds of death and birth;
And sad at heart, for sorrow and sin,

We wondered, where might help begin.
And on our wonder came God's choice,
A sudden light, a clarion voice,
Clearing the dark, and sounding clear:
And we obeyed: behold us, here!
In prison bound, but with your chains:
Sufferers, but of alien pains.
Merry the world, and thrives apace,
Each in his customary place:
Sailors upon the carrying sea,
Shepherds upon the pasture lea,
And merchants of the town; and they,
Who march to death, the fighting way;
And there are lovers in the spring,
With those, who dance, and those, who sing:
The commonwealth of every day,
Eastward and westward, far away,
Once the sun paled; once cried aloud
The Roman, from beneath the cloud:
This day the Son of God is dead!
Yet heed men, what the Roman said?
They heed not: we then heed for them,
The mindless of Jerusalem;
Careless, they live and die: but we
Care, in their stead, for Calvary.
O joyous men and women! strong,
To urge the wheel of life along,
With strenuous arm, and cheerful strain,
And wisdom of laborous brain:

We give our life, our heart, our breath,
That you may live to conquer death;
That, past your tomb, with souls in health,
Joy may be yours, and blessed wealth;
Through vigils of the painful night,
Our spirits with your tempters fight:
For you, for you, we live alone,
Where no joy comes, where cold winds moan:
Nor friends have we, nor have we foes;
Our Queen is of the lonely Snows.
Ah! and sometimes, our prayers between,
Come sudden thoughts of what hath been:
Dreams! And from dreams, once more we fall
To prayer: *God save, Christ keep, them all.*
And thou, who knowest not these things,
Hearken, what news our message brings!
Our toils, thy joy of life forgot:
Our lives of prayer forget thee not.

CADGWITH

By LIONEL JOHNSON

My windows open to the autumn night,
In vain I watched for sleep to visit me:
How should sleep dull mine ears, and dim my sight,
Who saw the stars, and listened to the sea?

Ah, how the City of our God is fair!
If, without sea and starless though it be,
For joy of the majestic beauty there,
Men shall not miss the stars, nor mourn the sea.

A FRIEND

By LIONEL JOHNSON

All, that he came to give,
He gave, and went again:
I have seen one man live,
I have seen one man reign,
With all the graces in his train.

As one of us, he wrought
Things of the common hour:
Whence was the charmed soul brought,
That gave each act such power;
The natural beauty of a flower?

Magnificence and grace,
Excellent courtesy:
A brightness on the face,
Airs of high memory:
Whence came all these, to such as he?

Like young Shakespearian kings,
He won the adoring throng:
And, as Apollo sings,
He triumphed with a song:
Triumphed, and sang, and passed along.

With a light word he took
The hearts of men in thrall:
And, with a golden look,
Welcomed them, at his call
Giving their love, their strength, their all.

No man less proud than he,
Nor cared for homage less;
Only, he could not be
Far off from happiness:
Nature was bound to his success.

Weary, the cares, the jars
The lets, of every day:
But the heavens filled with stars,
Chanced he upon the way:
And where he stayed, all joy would stay.

Now, when sad night draws down,
When the austere stars burn:
Roaming the vast stars burn:
My thoughts and memories yearn
Toward him, who never will return.

Yet I have seen him live,
And owned my friend, a king:
And that he came to give,
He gave, and I, who sing
His praise, bring all I have to bring.

BY THE STATUE OF KING CHARLES
AT CHARING CROSS

By LIONEL JOHNSON

Sombre and rich, the skies;
 Great glooms and starry plains.
Gently the night wind sighs;
 Else a vast silence reigns.

The splendid silence clings
 Around me: and around
The saddest of all kings
 Crowned, and again discrowned.

Comely and calm, he rides
 Hard by his own Whitehall:
Only the night wind glides:
 No crowds, nor rebels, brawl.

Gone, too, his Court: and yet,
  The stars his courtiers are;
Stars in their stations set;
  And every wandering star.

Alone he rides, alone,
  The fair and fatal king:
Dark night is all his own,
  That strange and solemn thing.

Which are more full of fate:
  The stars; or those sad eyes?
Which are more still and great:
  Those brows; or the dark skies?

Although his whole heart yearn
  In passionate tragedy:
Never was face so stern
  With sweet austerity.

Vanquished in life, his death
  By beauty made amends:
The passing of his breath
  Won his defeated ends.

Brief life, and hapless? Nay:
  Through death, life grew sublime.
Speak after sentence? Yea:
  And to the end of time.

Armoured he rides, his head
　　Bare to the stars of doom:
He triumphs now, the dead,
　　Beholding London's gloom.

Our wearier spirit faints,
　　Vexed in the world's employ:
His soul was of the saints;
　　And art to him was joy.

King, tried in fires of woe!
　　Men hunger for thy grace:
And through the night I go,
　　Loving thy mournful face.

Yet, when the city sleeps;
　　When all the cries are still:
The stars and heavenly deeps
　　Work out a perfect will.

THE HOUSEWIFE'S PRAYER

By BLANCHE MARY KELLY

Lady, who with tender word
Didst keep the house of Christ the Lord,
Who didst set forth the bread and wine

Before the Living Wheat and Vine,
Reverently didst make the bed
Whereon was laid the holy Head
That such a cruel pillow prest
For our behoof, on Calvary's crest;
Be beside me while I go
About my labors to and fro.
Speed the wheel and speed the loom,
Guide the needle and the broom,
Make my bread rise sweet and light,
Make my cheese come foamy white,
Yellow may my butter be
As cowslips blowing on the lea.
Homely though my tasks and small,
Be beside me at them all.
Then when I shall stand to face
Jesu in the judgment place,
To me thy gracious help afford,
Who art the Handmaid of the Lord.

BROTHER JUNIPER

By BLANCHE MARY KELLY

As unto Francis Poverty,
So Folly was a bride to thee.
Not the jade that fashions quips

For the smiles of mocking lips,
And in the face of stony Death
Capers till she's out of breath,
But the maid that moves and sings
About divinely foolish things,
She that gives her substance all
For love, and laughs to find it small,
She that drew God's Son to be
A butt, a jest on Calvary,
And 'neath the leper's guise doth know
The King in his incognito.
The world is grown too wise, and we
Go our sad ways sensibly.
O, would that our lean souls might win
Some grace of thine, God's harlequin,
Whose days were lavished like fool's gold
Upon His pleasures manifold.
"Would God," cried Francis, on his knees,
"I had a forest of such trees!"

THE THRONE OF THE KING

By FRANCIS CLEMENT KELLEY

The sun was setting, and its golden glow
Deepened the shadows on the village street,
And reverent touched the beauty of the head

Of Him who sat, in thought, beside the well
Of Nazareth. Two women came to fill
Their earthen jars; and sent their burdens down
To where the water lay; then drew them up.
But still the Boy, unmoved, gazed steadily
Upon the distant hills, that girded round
Jerusalem, the City of the Soul.

His eyes were deep as some unfathomed sea,
That tosses wreckage on its billowed crest;
But hides its treasures ever in the caves,
That men shall never touch, or touching die.
"How strange the Boy," one woman softly said
As back they went, their burdens on their heads.
"Yet He is Joseph's Son," the other spoke,
"And Joseph is my neighbor, a just man;
But not more lettered than the other men,
Your own and mine. He is not priest nor scribe
That he could teach such wisdom to his Son.
And it doth sometimes seem the Boy is wise
Beyond His years, with knowledge overmuch."
"His mother, whom I know," her friend replied,
"As Mary, sweeps the shavings from the floor,
Cooks the poor fare for Joseph and her Son,
Cares for the water, and her jar brings here
As we do every day, who know not much
Beyond the things we hear from holy men.
Yet strange is Mary too; I know not where
To match the peace that's on her tranquil brow;

Though, through it all, I've seen the Shadow there
The dread of days to come, though all resigned.
So like His mother is this only Son
In beauty, in the peace that's on His face;
But sometimes, deeper still, the Shadow falls
Across His features. Look! behold it now.
For it doth speak the dread of awful things,
More awful than the ruin of a world!"

A-down the street there rang a clatter loud
Of horses dashing in a maddened run,
And sounds of wheels swift rolling on the pave.
The women shrank affrighted to the wall,
And cowered there in trembling, mortal fear.
In view the charging horses passed along
Straight to the well, no driver grasped the reins,
For he had fallen to the stony street.
Yet never moved the Boy, nor turned His eyes
From off the hills that held them so intent.
But from a doorway rushed a stranger lad
Who grasped the bit of one, and held him fast.
The others, panting, stopped so near the Boy
That, on His face He must have felt the heat
Which steaming rose from their perspiring flanks,
As now they stood, foam-flecked and trembling by.
The driver came and meekly murmured thanks,
Before he led his charges back again
To where his master waited for the steeds.
"He gave me naught but words, and I did save

The steeds. The chariot, too, would have been dashed
All broken on the stones, had I not come."
The lad was angered, but the Boy moved not,
Though from the distant hills His gaze was drawn.
"Dost thou not know," the lad said, wonderingly,
"How near was Death to thee a moment since?"

The Boy, now fully aroused, smiled at the lad
All kindly, as a loving father smiles
Upon his child that waked him unaware,
Whose sleep nor storm nor clatter could affect,
Yet at the touch of little baby hands
Opens wide his eyes, that twinkle joyfully.
"No nearer to grim Death," the Boy replied,
"Was I than thou, my friend, art near it now.
Thou seekest Joseph and hast wandered far
From distant Jaffa, where thy father died.
Thou'rt Fidus named. From Joseph thou wouldst learn
The craftsman's art, and how to handle tools
To work with wood, that thou thyself may'st be
Like him, a craftsman skilled in his own trade."
"A prophet Thou!" the lad in wonder cried.
"Come with me," made He answer. "I am known
As Joseph's Son; so I will speak for thee."

As evening fell on Nazareth's burning street
Each day these two would wander out alone;
And by the well, or in a quiet glade
Seated, would hold their talk, with none to hear.

Yet converse scarce it was; with ears intent,
Fidus did always listen, while the Boy
Poured out a tale of Kings and Prophets old;
Of marvels that they worked to testify
Unto a King whom yet the earth would see,
A King of all Judea and the world;
Whose glory, mounting even to the stars
Would dim with rich effulgence, their great light.
The Sun of Justice He, the Moon of night
That had for ages settled o'er the earth.
He told of wonders that the King would do
Before He mounted to His mighty throne.
He told of love surpassing every love
That earth had seen, and of His Kingdom wide;
Till all on fire Fidus hung'red to see
The King Himself, and worship at His throne.
"A Roman though I am," he oft would cry,
"Thy King I'd welcome and for Him I'd serve."
"Yet thou art craftsman and no soldier thou."
"A craftsman too can serve his loyal due."
"How wouldst thou serve?" the Boy inquiring spoke.
"When Joseph bids me go, that I can learn no more,
This I can do—to build for Him His throne."

The Shadow swept across the boyish face—
The Shadow Fidus once had seen before;
And he was silent, for in awe he stood
When that mysterious shade shut off the light
That shone out from the radiant brow.

The Shadow was not fear, nor dread of death;
But dread of something worse than death could bring.
It was as if a lily, broken, bent,
But yet unsullied, now was stained with filth
By impious hand; more cruel far than death
The marring of the whiteness death had spared:
Or like a stream, that through its mountain bed
Had raced unfettered, toward the amber sea,
And o'er the rapids and the pebbles dashed
Clear, cold and placid when the mouth is reached;
Then, death unfeared before it, ready now
To give back to the ocean all it gave,
Into its pureness poured a stream so dark
That tainted all its life, when life was lost.
'Twas thus the Shadow seemed; but soon it passed,
And smiling boyhood turned a happy face
The while he said: "So thou wouldst build His throne?
But dost thou know the form that throne will take?"

"'T will be a throne," Fidus replied, "so high
That all may see Him, while from it He reigns,
And know that He has come unto His own."

"Aye," quick the Boy made answer, "it shall be
Uplifted high that every man may see;
Not Jews alone but even ye of Rome;
And men from Britain too, on farthest shore
Of Rome's great Empire: they shall see and know
The King who reigns upon that living throne;

And in the Islands of unchartered seas
The King shall lifted be, that all may know;
And worlds still undiscovered shall bow down
To do Him homage, yet shall hate His name.
For homage goes with hate, and hate will be
The measure of the homage that shall swell
In pæans great around the royal throne."

Fidus looked wond'ring at the Boy Who spoke,
As if the right to build the throne were His
And He could give it to the friend who asked
This only boon, as pledge of love untold.

"And I would build it strong so it could go
O'er sea and land, and last for aye and aye."

"So thou wouldst build the throne?" again the Boy
Half musing spoke. Across His face once more
The Shadow fell; and, as he stood, His hands
He lifted up and out, as if in prayer.
Another Shadow fell upon the ground,
The arms and body strangely like a Cross.
Fidus was silent till the prayer was done.
The sun now set, and all the shadows passed.
They, arm in arm, ran fast to Joseph's house.
But, at the door they paused and, said the Boy:
"Thou must remember ever this thy day
When I the promise gave that I can keep,
For thou shalt build His throne!"

The years passed on,
And Fidus to the Roman hosts returned
Where, welcomed as a soldier's clever son,
He wrought in wood for all the legions there
In Jaffa, where his father had been killed.
For eighteen years he stayed beside the sea
And, working at the trade that Joseph taught,
He never once forgot the precious pledge
The Boy had made. But never saw nor heard
Aught of his friend. Then he was sent away
By Pilate's call, unto Jerusalem.

The evening of the day when he arrived
Great turmoil swept along the Jaffa road,
And near the Gate of Gardens, where the hill
Called Calvary lifted up its rocky head.
He heard the crowds discuss a Wonder-Man
The priests had taken, and was on His way
To judgment. "Out on such a King," cried one,
"Himself He can not save from shameful death.
Tomorrow's sun will see Him lifted up
Above the hill, and throw the Shadow of
A Cross upon you fools who thought Him King."

And on the faces dark of all around,
Fidus saw Hate he could not understand.
Then up a vision rose of Nazareth
When evening fell; a Boy of beauty rare,
With a strange Shadow on His lovely face,

Standing with arms outstretched in prayer,
The glory of the setting sun upon His head.
But long and grim the shadow of a Cross
Before Him as He stood. Then to his mind
Came swift the stories of the mighty King,
And then the promise: "Thou shalt build His throne."

Alas! the long and wav'ring years had swept
The dreams of youth away; but still remained
The love, that hungered now to feel the hand
Within his own of Mary's Son. The day
Rose brightly in the East. At Pilate's door
He met by chance a captain he had known
In Jaffa, who bade him attentive wait
Within the hall, amongst the soldiers there.
But soon a tumult rose without the doors;
The Wonder-Man was coming to be judged.
Then, as the cries increased, his friend came in.
"Make thou a Cross," he said, "We have but two
And, if I judge aright, three shall be sent
Beyond the wall this day to Calvary."

No more of shouting Fidus heard, for he
Alone made ready a great Cross of wood;
And, that his craftsman skill should be confessed,
He made it well, both strong and workmanlike.
"'Tis fit," he said, "to serve a King," and smiled
At his grim jest; then went he on his way.

Out in the streets the crowd was surging on
Along the way that leads to Calvary's hill.
And o'er it Fidus saw his Cross; and then,
Sometimes, a thorn-crowned head with waving hair
Blood-clotted now, and stained a deeper hue;
And Hate seemed in the air vibrating round.
When sudden, like a bell that sweetly rings
Above a storm, and seems a messenger
Of Peace and Love, there woke upon his soul
From out the sleeping past, some prophet words:
"For homage goes with hate, and hate shall be
The measure of the homage that shall swell
In pæans great around the royal throne."

The surging crowd hid from his eyes the things
He did not care to see, but faint he heard
The hammer strokes, that seemed to drive the nails
Deep in his heart. Then turned he to a man
Who silent stood beside him, and he said:
"A stranger I, from Jaffa, yesternight
I came. This man? What evil hath He done?"
"I know not any wrong that He hath done,"

Came answer fast. "I only know the good
That He had wrought. Behold my eyes that see!
Once they were dark. He passed me by one day
And loud I cried: 'O Son of David, mercy show
That I may see.' He touched me and I saw."
Another silent man near Fidus stood,

To him he spoke, "And friend, what knowest thou?"
"I know that now I live though I was dead;
For I had gone into the ending tomb
All spiced for rest and bound with linen bands;
And He did come, and He did call me forth.
I heard His voice that sounded far away,
As if I stood within a valley deep,
And some one, from the mountain crest,
Kept calling me. Then clearer was the Voice;
As if on wings, I soared aloft to Him,
Who had the Power to bid me come or stay.
Again my heart did beat and vital blood
Surged through my wid'ning veins. I lived again."

Then Fidus quick recalled a wondrous thing:
He saw the Boy in Joseph's little shop,
A sick lamb refuged in His tender arms.
He gently stroked the lamb and then the pain
Was gone from out its piteous pleading eyes.
And, lo, the man felt hot tears on his cheeks.

The Cross was raised, and faint the outline stood
'Twixt Fidus and the lurid, murky sky
That threatened from afar a terror dark.
Then swift it came, for all of darkness dread
That air could hold, fell down upon the earth.
The stumbling crowd in panic slunk away;
But Fidus groped through darkness to the Cross.

He heard a moan of sorrow. Well he knew
The voice of Mary, she of Joseph's house.
His heart stood still; the Vision came again:
That evening fair—the Boy—the distant hills—
The Shadow of the Cross upon the earth
As He stood silent all absorbed in prayer—
The promise that himself should build a throne.
"Aye," so the Boy had said, "for it shall be
Raised up on high that every man may see,
Not Jews alone, but even ye of Rome;
And men from Britain too, on farthest shore
Of Rome's great Empire: they shall see and know
The King Who reigns upon that living throne;
And, in the Islands of uncharted seas
The King shall lifted be that all may know;
And worlds still undiscovered shall bow down
To do Him homage, yet shall hate His name.
For homage goes with hate, and hate will be
The measure of the homage that shall swell
In pæans great around His royal throne."

A lightning flash! The rocks asunder rent,
The tombs burst open and the dead arose.
One moment Fidus saw the Crucified
Ere darkness fell again around the Cross.
But in that moment a new vision rose;
He saw the hill rise high, and higher still,
Till over all the mountains of the world
It towering stood; and nations, worshipping

Gazed on a mighty throne that bore a King!
Blood red the jewels in His crown of thorns,
With ermined pain that wrapped Him all about,
Deep in His hands the orb and sceptre nails,
Quite gone the Shadow of the primal sin
And, on His brow, fulfilled the ancient pledge
Of Earth's Redemption.

THE CHILD'S WISH GRANTED

By GEORGE PARSONS LATHROP

Do you remember, my sweet, absent son,
How in the soft June days forever done
You loved the heavens so warm and clear and high;
And, when I lifted you, soft came your cry—
"Put me 'way up—'way up in blue sky"?

I laughed and said I could not—set you down
Your gray eyes wonder-filled beneath that crown
Of bright hair gladdening me as your raced by,
Another Father now, more strong than I,
Has borne you voiceless to your dear blue sky.

CHARITY

By GEORGE PARSONS LATHROP

Unarmed she goeth, yet her hands
Strike deeper awe than steel-caparisoned bands,
No fatal hurt of foe she fears—
Veiled, as with mail, in mist of gentle tears.

'Gainst her thou canst not bar the door;
Like air she enters; where none dared before.
Even to the rich she can forgive
Their regal selfishness—and let them live!

A SONG BEFORE GRIEF

By ROSE HAWTHORNE LATHROP

Sorrow, my friend,
When shall you come again?
The wind is slow, and the bent willows send
Their silvery motions wearily down the plain.
The bird is dead
That sang this morning through the summer rain!

Sorrow, my friend,
I owe my soul to you.

And if my life with any glory end
Of tenderness for others, and the words are true,
Said, honoring, when I'm dead—
Sorrow, to you, the mellow praise, the funeral wreath,
  are due.

And yet, my friend,
When love and joy are strong,
Your terrible visage from my sight I rend
With glances to blue heaven. Hovering along,
By mine your shadow led,
"Away!" I shriek, "nor dare to work my new-sprung
  mercies wrong!"

Still, you are near:
Who can your care withstand?
When deep eternity shall look most clear,
Sending bright waves to kiss the trembling land,
My joy shall disappear—
A flaming torch thrown to the golden sea by your pale hand.

THE CLOCK'S SONG

By ROSE HAWTHORNE LATHROP

Eileen of four,
Eileen of smiles;

Eileen of five,
Eileen of tears;
Eileen of ten, of fifteen years,
Eileen of youth
And woman's wiles;
Eileen of twenty,
In love's land,
Eileen all tender
In her bliss,
Untouched by sorrow's treacherous kiss,
And the sly weapons in life's hand—
Eileen aroused to share all fate,
Eileen a wife,
Pale, beautiful,
Eileen most grave and dutiful,
Mourning her dreams in queenly state.
Eileen! Eileen! …

IRELAND

By EDMUND LEAMY (SENIOR)

I loved a love—a royal love—
  In the golden long ago;
And she was fair as fair could be.
The foam upon the broken sea,
The sheen of sun, or moon, or star,

The sparkle from the diamond spar,
Not half so rare and radiant are
   As my own love—my royal love—
     In the golden long ago.

And she had stately palace halls—
   In the golden long ago;
And warriors, men of stainless swords,
Were seated at her festive boards,
Fierce champions of her lightest words,
While hymned the bard the chieftain's praise,
And sang their deed of battle days,
   To cheer my love, my royal love,
     In the golden long ago.

She wore a stately diadem—
   In the golden long ago;
Wrought by a cunning craftsman's hand,
And fashioned from a battle brand,
Full fit for the queen of a soldier land;
Her sceptre was a sabre keen,
Her robe a robe of radiant green,
   My queenly love, my royal love,
     In the golden long ago.

Alas for my love, my royal love,
   Of the golden long ago!
For gone are all her warrior bands,
And rusted are her battle brands,

And broken her sabre bright and keen,
And torn her robe of radiant green,
A slave where she was a stainless queen,
   My own love, my royal love,
      Of the golden long ago.

But there is hope for my royal love
Of the golden long ago;
Beyond the broad and shining sea
Gathers a stubborn chivalry,
That yet will come to make her free,
And hedge her round with gleaming spears,
And crown her queen of all the years,
   My own love, my royal love,
      Of the golden long ago.

MUSIC MAGIC

By EDMUND LEAMY

Perhaps there is no magic in this dull old world of ours;
Perhaps there are no Fairy Tales to gladden heart-break hours;
Perhaps there is no beauty, and perhaps all things are wrong;
But still there is the wonder of a little, old-time song!
A squeaking and battered old organ, rattling a
  moss-covered tune,
Stood in the street of the city, there, in the heat of the noon;

Banging of roses and sunshine, thrilling of lands far away,
Whispering songs of my childhood—sorrowful, simple
  and gay;
I was a child for a moment, filled with a child's petty fears,
Dreaming, and dreaming, and dreaming, never a thought
  of the tears.
Then as the music softened, singing of love and of life,
Brought it back thought of the old days, far from the toil
  and the strife,
Glimmer of gold in the star-light, shimmer of silk by the sea;
Words that were whispered, half-spoken, dreams that were
  never to be.
Sweet intermingled with sadness, what is as dear as the past?
Is there a day in the future that is as fair as the last?
Music, oh, music the master, there in the heat of the noon,
A squeaking and battered old organ, rattling a
  moss-covered tune,
Carried me back in my dreaming, far, to the long, long ago;
Feeling, 'way down in my heart-chords, hope I thought never
  could glow;
Brought to me, who was a failure, beaten and crossed in
  the fight,
Help in the hour of the darkness—pointed the way to
  the light.
Perhaps there is no magic in this dull, old world of ours;
Perhaps there are no Fairy Tales to gladden heart-break hours;
Perhaps there is no beauty and perhaps all things are wrong;
But still there is the wonder of a little, old-time song!

GETHSEMANE

By Edmund Leamy

Breathes there a man who claimeth not
  One lonely spot,
    His own Gethsemane,
Whither with his inmost pain
  He fain
    Would weary plod,
Find the surcease that is known
  In wind a-moan
    And sobbing sea,
Cry his sorrow hid of men,
  And then—
    Touch hands with God.

MY LIPS WOULD SING—

By Edmund Leamy (senior)

My lips would sing a song for you, a soulful little song
  for you,
  A plaintive little song for you, upon a summer's day;
But for the very life of me, the merry, merry life of me,
  The laughter-loving life of me, I cannot but be gay.

For oh, the sun is shining, Dear, and who could be repining,
Dear,
And who would be unhappy, Dear, when all the world
is young?
So I will hum a melody, a mirthful little melody,
A joyous little melody that never yet was sung.

And you shall hear of Fairyland, of Kings and Queens of
Fairyland,
Of men and maids of Fairyland, and Love shall be
the theme,
And straight before your brimming eyes, a golden glint
of Paradise
Shall steal, My Dear, to still your sighs, and give you back
your dream.

And you will taste of happiness, a tiny bit of happiness,
A wistful bit of happiness, upon a summer's day;
And just a little smile from you, a sunny little smile from you,
A trembly little smile from you shall be a poet's pay!

MY SHIP

By EDMUND LEAMY

My ship is an old ship and her sails are grey and torn,
And in the dim and misty night she seems a thing forlorn;

Her battered sides are beetle black, her decks are scarred and
old,
And heavy rise the musty scents from out her crumbling
hold.

The young ships in the tide-way with a sneering smile sail by,
And fair they flash their white sails against a sun-drenched sky,
And fleet they run before the clouds that usher in a blow,
But could a storm coerce my ship whene'er she wished to go!

My ship is an old ship and her sails are torn and grey,
And she's not white and beautiful, nor fragile such as they,
But she has sailed o'er every sea to every land a-gleam,
And on her decks make merry now the wraiths of youthful
dream!

VISIONS

By EDMUND LEAMY

I never watch the sun set a-down the Western skies
But that within its wonderness I see my mother's eyes;
I never hear the West wind sob softly in the trees
But that there comes her broken call far o'er the distant seas;
And never shine the dim stars but that my heart would go
Away and back to olden lands and dreams of long ago.

A rover of the wide world, when yet my heart was young
The sea came whispering to me in well-beloved tongue,
And oh! the promises she held of golden lands a-gleam
That clung about my boy-heart and filled mine eyes with
    dream,
And Wanderlust came luring me till 'neath the stars I swore
That I would be a wanderer for ever, ever more.

A-rover of the wide world, I've seen the Northern lights
A-flashing countless colours in the knife-cold wintry nights;
I've watched the Southern Cross ablaze o'er smiling, sunny
    lands,
And seen the lazy sea caress palm-sheltered, silvery sands;
Still wild unrest is scouring me, the Wanderlust of yore,
And I must be a wanderer for ever, ever more.

And yet, I see the sun set a-down the Western skies
And glimpse within the wonderness my mother's pleading eyes;
And yet I hear the West wind sob softly in the trees,
That vainly cloaks her broken call far o'er the distant seas;
And still when shine the dim stars my wander heart would go
Away and back to her side, and dreams of long ago.

IRELAND, MOTHER OF PRIESTS

By SHANE LESLIE

The fishwife sits by the side
Of her childing bed,
Her fire is deserted and sad,
Her beads are long said;
Her tears ebb and flow with the sea,
Her grief on the years,
But little she looks to the tide,
And little she hears:
For children in springtime play round
Her sorrowing heart,
To win them their feeding she loves
To hunger apart;
Her children in summer she counts
Awhile for her own;
But winter is ever the same,
The loved ones are flown.
Far over the sea they are gone,
Far out of her ken
They travel the furthest of seas
As fishers of men.
Yet never a word to her sons
To keep them at home,
And never a motherly cry
Goes over the foam;
She sits with her head in her hands,

Her eyes on the flame,
And thinks of the others that played,
Yet left her the same,
With vesture she wove on the loom
Four-coloured to be,
And lanterns she trimmed with her hair
To light them to sea.
Oh, far have the living ones gone,
And further the dead,
For spirits come never to watch
The fisherwife's bed;
And sonless she sits at the hearth,
And peers in the flame,
She knows that their fishing must come
As ever it came—
A fishing that never set home,
But seaways it led,
For God who has taken her sons
Has buried her dead.

THE HUNTERS

By RUTH TEMPLE LINDSAY

"The Devil, as a roaring lion, goeth about seeking whom
he may devour."

The Lion, he prowleth far and near.
  Nor swerves for pain or rue;
He heedeth nought of sloth nor fear,
  He prowleth—prowleth through
The silent glade and the weary street,
  In the empty dark and the full noon heat;
And a little Lamb with aching feet—
  He prowleth too.

The Lion croucheth alert, apart—
  With patience doth he woo;
He waiteth long by this shuttered heart,
  And the Lamb—He waiteth too.
Up the lurid passes of dreams that kill,
  Through the twisting maze of the great Untrue,
The Lion followeth the fainting will—
  And the Lamb—He followeth too.

From the tickets dim of the hidden way
  Where the debts of Hell accrue,
The Lion leapeth upon his prey:
  But the Lamb—He leapeth too.
Ah! loose the leash of the sins that damn,
  Mark Devil and God as goals,
In the panting love of a famished Lamb,
  Gone mad with the need of souls.

The Lion, he strayeth near and far;
  What heights hath he left untrod?

He crawleth nigh to the purest star,
  On the trail of the saints of God.
And throughout the darkness of things unclean,
  In the depths where the sin-ghouls brood,
There prowleth ever with yearning mien—
  A lamb as white as Blood!

IN CHERRY LANE

By Rev. William Livingston

In Cherry Lane the blossoms blow
  In wreaths of white around the trees,
And spread their petals wide, as though
  They longed for nectar-seeking bees.

O'erhead, the arching boughs that spring
  From pillar trunks look down and smile
On lowly currant shrubs that cling
  Around their feet along the aisle.

In Cherry Lane the sunbeams steal
  Through many a leaf and branch above,
And tender shoots come forth to feel
  The touches of a wondrous love.

And life grows warmer with the hours,
    Unmoved, unchilled by human pang,
Till from the stems now robed in flowers
    The great red drops in clusters hang.

Ah, Mother mine! white blossoms came
    And filled my soul with thoughts of thee,
Who art to those that love thy name
    What honeyed buds are to the bee.

Thou art the floweret white and fair,
    A virgin from thy stainless birth,
The fruitful stem designed to bear
    A Saviour to our sinful earth.

And when the cherries, ripe and red,
    Come forth upon the breast of June,
They'll tell me of a heart that bled,
    By men forgotten all too soon.

Ah, precious drops! through future days
    Preserve my soul from spot or stain,
With tender thoughts of love and praise
    That once were mine in Cherry Lane.

SURRENDER

By S. M. M.

If thou art merely conscious clay—ah, well,
  Tire not such stuff with futile, tread-mill climb
  Which lifts to leave thee level with the slime;
Nor think that death can break thy earth-born spell;
  Clay hath no heel Achillean, vulnerable.
  Be animate till some deliberate time
Shall choke and crunch thee to potential grime,
For thou art fit for neither heaven nor hell.

But He Who made thee cousin to the clod
  First plunged thee in the Spirit Which is He,
Whence thou hast risen, divinely armed and shod
  To scale the ramparts of eternity.
Already stricken with the shafts of God,
  Thou fallest prisoner to the Deity.

HYMN FOR PENTECOST

By James Clarence Mangan

Pure Spirit of the always-faithful God,
Kindler of Heaven's true light within the soul!
From the lorn land our sainted fathers trod,

Ascends to Thee our cry of hope and dole.
Thee, Thee we praise;
To Thee we raise
Our choral hymn in these awakening days:
O send us down anew that fire
Which of old lived in David's and Isaiah's lyre.

Centuries had rolled, and earth lay tombed in sleep,
The nightmare-sleep of nations beneath kings;
And far abroad o'er liberty's great deep
Death's angel waved his black and stilling wings.
Then struck Thine hour!
Thou, in Thy power,
But breathedst, and the free stood up, a tower;
And tyranny's thrones and strongholds fell,
And men made jubilee for an abolished hell.

And she, our mother-home, the famed, the fair,
The golden house of light and intellect,
Must she still groan in her intense despair?
Shall she lie prone while Europe stands erect?
Forfend this, Thou
To whom we vow
Souls even our giant wrongs shall never bow:
Thou wilt not leave our green flag furled,
Nor bear that we abide the byword of the world.

Like the last lamp that burned in Tullia's tomb
Through ages, vainly, with unwaning ray;

Our star of hope lights but a path of gloom
Whose false track leads us round and round alway.
But Thou canst open
A gate from hope
To victory! Thou canst nerve our arms to cope
With looming storm and danger still,
And lend a thunder-voice to the land's lightning will.

Descend, then, Spirit of the Eternal King!
To Thee, to Him, to His avenging Son,
The Triune of God, in boundless trust we cling;
His help once ours, our nationhood is won.
We watch the time
Till that sublime
Event shall thrill the free of every clime.
Speed, mighty Spirit! speed its march,
And thus complete for earth mankind's triumphal arch.

DARK ROSALEEN

By JAMES CLARENCE MANGAN

O my dark Rosaleen,
    Do not sigh, do not weep!
The priests are on the ocean green,
    They march along the deep.

There's wine from the royal Pope
  Upon the ocean green,
And Spanish ale shall give you hope,
  My dark Rosaleen!
  My own Rosaleen!
Shall glad your heart, shall give you hope,
Shall give you health, and help, and hope,
  My dark Rosaleen!

Over hills and through dales
  Have I roamed for your sake;
All yesterday I sailed the sails
  On river and on lake.
The Erne, at its highest flood,
  I dashed across unseen,
For there was lightning in my blood,
  My dark Rosaleen!
  My own Rosaleen!
Oh! there was lightning in my blood,
Red lightning through my blood,
  My dark Rosaleen!

All day long, in unrest,
  To and fro do I move,
The very soul within my breast
  Is wasted for you, love!
The heart in my bosom faints
  To think of you, my Queen,
My life of life, my saint of saints,

My dark Rosaleen!
My own Rosaleen!
To hear your sweet and sad complaints,
My life, my love, my saint of saints,
    My dark Rosaleen!

Woe and pain, pain and woe,
    Are my lot, night and noon,
To see your bright face clouded so,
    Like to the mournful moon.
But yet will I rear your throne
    Again in golden sheen;
'Tis you shall reign, shall reign alone,
    My dark Rosaleen!
    My own Rosaleen!
'Tis you shall have the golden throne,
'Tis you shall reign, and reign alone,
    My dark Rosaleen!

Over dews, over sands,
    Will I fly for your weal:
Your holy, delicate white hands
    Shall girdle me with steel.
At home in your emerald bowers,
    From morning's dawn till e'en,
You'll pray for me, my flower of flowers,
    My dark Rosaleen!
    My own Rosaleen!
You'll think of me through daylight's hours,

My virgin flower, my flower of flowers,
  My dark Rosaleen!

I could scale the blue air,
  I could plough the high hills,
Oh, I could kneel all night in prayer,
  To heal your many ills!
And one beamy smile from you
  Would float like light between
My toils and me, my own, my true,
  My dark Rosaleen!
  My own Rosaleen!
Would give me life and soul anew,
A second life, a soul anew,
  My dark Rosaleen!

Oh! the Erne shall run red
  With redundance of blood,
The earth shall rock beneath our tread,
  And flames wrap hill and wood,
And gun-peal and slogan-cry
  Wake many a glen serene,
Ere you shall fade, ere you shall die,
  My dark Rosaleen!
  My own Rosaleen!
The Judgment Hour must first be nigh,
Ere you shall fade, ere you can die,
  My dark Rosaleen!

WHAT IS WHITE?

By THOMAS MACDONAGH

What is white?
  The soul of the sage, faith-lit,
The trust of Age,
  The infant's untaught wit.
What more white?
  The face of Truth made known,
The Voice of Youth
  Singing before her throne.

WISHES FOR MY SON
BORN ON ST. CECILIA'S DAY, 1912

By THOMAS MACDONAGH

Now, my son, is life for you—
And I wish you joy of it—
Joy of power in all you do,
Deeper passion, better wit
Than I had who had enough,
Quicker life and length thereof,
More of every gift but love.

Love I have beyond all men,
Love that now you share with me—
What have I to wish you then
But that you be good and free,
And that God to you may give
Grace in stronger days to live?

For I wish you more than I
Ever knew of glorious deed,
Though no rapture passed me by
That an eager heart could heed,
Though I followed heights and sought
Things the sequel never brought.

Wild and perilous holy things
Flaming with a martyr's blood,
And the joy that laughs and sings
Where a foe must be withstood,
Joy of headlong happy chance
Leading on the battle dance.

But I found no enemy,
No man in a world of wrong,
That Christ's word of Charity
Did not render clean and strong—
Who was I to judge my kind,
Blindest groper of the blind?

God to you may give the sight
And the clear undoubting strength
Wars to knit for single right,
Freedom's war to knit at length,
And to win, through wrath and strife,
To the sequel of my life.

But for you, so small and young,
Born on Saint Cecilia's Day,
I in more harmonious song
Now for nearer joys should pray—
Simple joys: the natural growth
Of your childhood and your youth,
Courage, innocence and truth:

These for you, so small and young,
In your hand and heart and tongue.

RESIGNATION

By SEUMAS MACMANUS

Be still, sad soul, be still,
Bend you to Heaven's high will.
When the toilsome race is run,
And the summit strove for won—
When secrets are unsealed,

All hidden things revealed,
All mysteries made known,
The good we doubted shown,
Vexed questionings at rest,
I'll say, "Well, God knew best."

.   .   .   .

Me thought you went full soon,
In the rapture of the noon,
In the glory of the sun,
Your noble work begun—
In your grasp the magic wand
That would raise a stricken land—
A while you fain would stay;
But the call brooked no delay:
You sighed, and bowed your head,
And they put you with the dead.

Our God is kind, and He
Will blunt the shaft to me;
Will stay the dripping woe
Ere the chalice overflow;
May let me end the race
With the high sun on my face,
And the hot blood bounding free,
Through the beating veins of me.
At most but some sad hours
And He'll call me when Night lowers.

Oh, at the Trysting Gate,
With radiant face you'll wait!
With arms in love outspread
To take a weary head,
And clasp it to your breast
Where always it found rest.
You'll speak no word for joy,
But, crooning o'er your boy,
Draw him into the Light,
Where nevermore comes Night.

IN DARK HOUR

By SEUMAS MACMANUS

I turn my steps where the Lonely Road
   Winds far as the eye can see,
And I bend my back for the burden sore
   That God has reached down to me.

I have said farewell to the sun-kissed plains,
   To joy I gave good-bye;
Now the bleak wide wastes of the world are mine,
   And the winds that wail in the sky.

No bright flower blooms, no sweet bird calls,
   Nor hermit ever abode,

Not a green thing lifts one lowly leaf,
  O God, on the Lonely Road!

The thick dank mists come stealing down,
  And press me on every side.
With never a voice to cheer me on,
  And never a hand to guide.

I shall cry in my need for a Voice and Hand,
  And the solace of love-wet eyes—
And an icy clutch will close on my heart,
  When Echo, the mocker, replies.

I know my good soul will fail me not,
  When Forms from the Dark round me creep,
And whisper 'twere sweet to journey no more,
  But lay down the burden and sleep.

(Look onward and up, O Heart of my Heart,
  Where the road strikes the skies afar!
To cheer you, and guide, thro' your darkest hour,
  Behold yon beckoning Star!)

I set my face to the grey wild wastes,
  I bend my back to the load—
Dear God be kind with the heart-sick child
  Who steps on the Lonely Road.

A SONG OF COLOURS

By THEODORE MAYNARD

Gold for the crown of Mary,
  Blue for the sea and sky,
Green for the woods and the meadows
  Where small white daisies lie,
And red for the colour of Christ's blood
  When He came to the cross to die.

These things the high God gave us
  And left in the world He made—
Gold for the hilt's enrichment,
  And blue for the sword's good blade,
And red for the roses a youth may set
  On the white brows of a maid.

Green for the cool, sweet gardens
  Which stretch about the house,
And the delicate new frondage
  The winds of spring arouse,
And red for the wine which a man may drink
  With his fellows in carouse.

Blue and green for the comfort
  Of tired hearts and eyes,
And red for that sudden hour which comes
  With danger and great surprise,

And white for the honour of God's throne
  When the dead shall all arise.

Gold for the cope and chalice,
  For kingly pomp and pride,
And red for the feathers men wear in their caps
  When they win a war or a bride,
And red for the robe which they dressed God in
  On the bitter day He died.

THE WORLD'S MISER

By THEODORE MAYNARD

I.

A miser with an eager face
Sees that each roseleaf is in place.

He keeps beneath strong bolts and bars
The piercing beauty of the stars.

The colours of the dying day
He hoards as treasure—well He may!—

And saves with care (lest they be lost)
The dainty diagrams of frost.

He counts the hairs of every head,
And grieves to see a sparrow dead.

II.

Among the yellow primroses
He holds His Summer palaces,

And sets the grass about them all
To guard them as His spearmen small.

He fixes on each wayside stone
A mark to show it as His own,

And knows when raindrops fall through air
Whether each single one be there,

That gathered into ponds and brooks.
They may become His picture books,

To show in every spot and place
The living glory of His face.

CECIDIT, CECIDIT BABYLON MAGNA!

By THEODORE MAYNARD

The aimless business of your feet,
  Your swinging wheels and piston rods,
The smoke of every sullen street
  Have passed away with all your Gods.

For in a meadow far from these
  A hodman treads across the loam,
Bearing his solid sanctities
  To that strange altar called his home.

I watch the tall, sagacious trees
  Turn as the monks do, every one;
The saplings, ardent novices,
  Turning with them towards the sun,

That Monstrance held in God's strong hands,
  Burnished in amber and in red;
God, His Own priest, in blessing stands;
  The earth, adoring, bows her head.

The idols of your market place,
  Your high debates, where are they now?
Your lawyers' clamour fades apace—
  A bird is singing on the bough!

Three fragile, sacramental things
　Endure, though all your pomps shall pass—
A butterfly's immortal wings,
　A daisy and a blade of grass.

A SONG OF LAUGHTER

By THEODORE MAYNARD

The stars with their laughter are shaken;
　The long waves laugh at sea;
And the little Imp of Laughter
　Laughs in the soul of me.

I know the guffaw of a tempest,
　The mirth of a blossom and bud—
But I laugh when I think of how Cuchulain laughed
　At the crows with their bills in his blood.

The mother laughs low at her baby,
　The bridegroom with joy in his bride—
And I think that Christ laughed when they took Him
　with staves
On the night before He died.

APOCALYPSE

By THEODORE MAYNARD

"And I saw a new heaven and a new earth: for the first heaven and the first earth are passed away" (Apoc. 21:1).

Shall summer wood where we have laughed our fill;
  Shall all your grass so good to walk upon;
Each field that we have loved, each little hill,
  Be burnt like paper—as hath said Saint John?

Then not alone they die! For God hath told
  How all His plains of mingled fire and glass,
His walls of hyacinth, His streets of gold,
  His aureoles of jewelled light shall pass,

That He may make us nobler things that these,
  And in her royal robes of blazing red
Adorn His bride. Yea, with what mysteries
  And might and mirth shall she be diamonded.

And what new secrets shall our God disclose;
  Or set what suns of burnished brass to flare;
Or what empurpled bloom to oust the rose;
  Or what strange grass to glow like angels' hair!

What pinnacles of silvery tracery,
  What dizzy, rampired towers shall God devise

Of topaz, beryl and chalcedony
  To make Heaven pleasant to His children's eyes!

And in what cataclysms of flame and foam
  Shall the first Heaven sink—as red as sin—
When God hath cast aside His ancient home
As far too mean to house His children in.

ST. BRIGID

By Denis A. McCarthy

Brigid, the daughter of Duffy, she wasn't like other
  young things,
Dreaming of lads for her lovers, and twirling her bracelets
  and rings;
Combing and coiling and curling her hair that was black as
  the sloes,
Painting her lips and her cheeks that were ruddy and fresh
  as the rose.
Ah, 'twasn't Brigid would waste all her days in such follies
  as these—
Christ was the Lover she worshipped for hour after hour on
  her knees;
Christ and His Church and His poor—and 'twas many a mile
  that she trod
Serving the loathsomest lepers that ever were stricken
  by God.

Brigid, the daughter of Duffy, she sold all her jewels
   and gems,
Sold all her finely-spun robes that were braided with gold to
   the hems;
Kept to her back but one garment, one dress that was faded
   and old,
Gave all her goods to the poor who were famished with
   hunger and cold.
Ah, 'twasn't Brigid would fling at the poor the hard word like
   a stone—
Christ the Redeemer she saw in each wretch that was ragged
   and lone;
Every wandering beggar who asked for a bite or a bed
Knocked at her heart like the Man who had nowhere to
   shelter His head.

Brigid, the daughter of Duffy, she angered her father at last.
"Where are your dresses, my daughter? Crom Cruach! You
   wear them out fast!
Where are the chains that I bought you all wrought in red
   gold from the mine?
Where the bright brooches of silver that once on your bosom
   would shine?"
Ah, but 'twas he was the man that was proud of his name and
   his race,
Proud of their prowess in battle and proud of their deeds in
   the chase!
Knew not the Christ, the pale God Whom the priests from
   afar had brought in,

Held to the old Gaelic gods that were known to Cuchullin
and Finn.

Brigid, the daughter of Duffy, made answer, "O father,"
said she,
"What is the richest of raiment, and what are bright jewels
to me?
Lepers of Christ must I care for, the hungry of Christ must
I feed;
How can I walk in rich robes when His people and mine are
in need?"
Ah, but 'twas she didn't fear for herself when he blustered
and swore,
Meekly she bowed when he ordered his chariot brought to
the door;
Meekly obeyed when he bade her get in at the point of
his sword,
Knowing whatever her fate she'd be safe with her Lover
and Lord.

Brigid, the daughter of Duffy, was brought to the court of
the King,
(Monarch of Leinster, MacEnda, whose praises the poets
would sing).
"Hither, O monarch," said Duffy, "I've come with a maiden
to sell;
Buy her and bind her to bondage—she's needing such
discipline well!"
Ah, but 'twas wise was the King. From the maid to the

chieftain he turned;
Mildness he saw in her face, in the other 'twas anger
    that burned;
"This is no bondmaid, I'll swear it, O chief, but a girl of
    your own.
Why sells the father the flesh of his flesh and the bone of
    his bone?"

Brigid, the daughter of Duffy, was mute while her father
    replied—
"Monarch, this maid has no place as the child of a chieftain
    of pride.
Beggars and wretches whose wounds would the soul of a
    soldier affright,
Sure, 'tis on these she is wasting my substance from morning
    till night!"
Ah, but 'twas bitter was Duffy; he spoke like a man that
    was vext.
Musing, the monarch was silent; he pondered the question
    perplexed.
"Maiden," said he, "if 'tis true, as I've just from your father
    heard tell,
Might it not be, as my bondmaid, you'd waste all my
    substance as well?"

Brigid, the daughter of Duffy, made answer. "O monarch,"
    she said,
"Had I the wealth from your coffers, and had I the crown
    from your head—

Yea, if the plentiful yield of the broad breasts of Erin
  were mine,
All would I give to the people of Christ who in poverty pine."
Ah, but 'twas then that the King felt the heart in his
  bosom upleap,
"I am not worthy," he cried, "such a maiden in bondage
  to keep!
Here's a king's sword for her ransom, and here's a king's word
  to decree
Never to other than Christ and His poor let her servitude be!"

ROSA MYSTICA

By DENIS A. McCARTHY

O Mystic Rose, in God's fair garden growing,
O Mystic Rose, in Heaven's high courtyard blowing—
Make sweet, make sweet the pathway I am going,
    O Mystic Rose!
The darkling, deathward way that I am going,
    O Mystic Rose!

O Rose, more white than snow-wreath in December!
O Rose, more red than sunset's dying ember,
My sins forget, my penitence remember,
    O Mystic Rose!

Though all should fail, I pray that thou remember,
    O Mystic Rose!

O Mystic Rose, the moments fly with fleetness;
To judgment I, with all my incompleteness—
But thou, make intercession by thy sweetness,
    O Mystic Rose!
Be near to soothe and save me by the sweetness,
    O Mystic Rose!

THE POOR MAN'S DAILY BREAD

By DENIS A. MCCARTHY

Not only there where jewelled vestments blaze,
    And princely prelates bow before Thy shrine,
Where myriads line the swept and garnished ways
    Through which is borne Thy Majesty Divine—
O Jesus of the ever loving heart,
    Not only there Thou art!

But where the lowliest church its cross uplifts
    Above the city's sordidness and sin;
Where all unheeded human wreckage drifts
    And drowns amid the foulness and the din—
There, too, anear the very gates of hell,
    O Saviour, dost Thou dwell!

Oh, meet it is that round Thy altar thrones,
　Thy highest priests should ministering throng
With silken robe, with gold and precious stones,
　With solemn chant and loud triumphant song:
What beauty that the world could give would be
　Too beautiful for Thee?

And yet to those that work with grimy hands
　And sweaty brows in ditches and in drains,
Thou comest with a love that understands
　Their labor ill-requitted, and their pains.
Who knows so well as Thou what they endure,
　O Father of the poor?

And so, deep-hid in many a city street,
　Or far where lonely workers break the soil,
Are shrines where Thou, the Merciful, dost meet,
　In love's embrace, the weary ones that toil.
For them Thy hospitable board is spread,
　With Thee, Thy very Self, their Daily Bread!

TO ASK OUR LADY'S PATRONAGE FOR A BOOK ON COLUMBUS: A FRAGMENT

By THOMAS D'ARCY MCGEE

Star of the Sea, to whom, age after age,
 The maiden kneels whose lover sails the sea;
Star, that the drowning death-pang can assuage,
 And shape the soul's course to eternity;
Mother of God, to Egypt's realm exiled,
 Mother of God, in Bethlehem's crib confined,
Thee do I ask to aid my anxious mind,
 And make this book find favour with thy Child.

Of one who lived and laboured in thy ray,
 I would rehearse the striving and success;
Through the dense past I ne'er shall find my way,
 Unless thou helpest, hold Comfortress;
A world of doubt and darkness to evade;
 An ocean all unknown to Christian kind;
Another world by nature's self arrayed,
 O'er the wide waste of waves, I seek to find.

A GENERAL COMMUNION

By ALICE MEYNELL

I saw the throng, so deeply separate,
　Fed at one only board—
The devout people, moved, intent, elate,
　And the devoted Lord.
Oh struck apart! not side from human side,
　But soul from human soul,
As each asunder absorbed the multiplied,
　The ever unparted whole.
I saw this people as a field of flowers,
　Each grown at such a price
The sum of unimaginable powers
　Did no more than suffice.
A thousand single central daisies they,
　A thousand of the one;
For each the entire monopoly of day;
　For each, the whole of the devoted sun.

THE SHEPHERDESS

By ALICE MEYNELL

She walks—the lady of my delight—
　A shepherdess of sheep.

Her flocks are thoughts. She keeps them white;
   She guards them from the steep;
She feeds them on the fragrant height,
   And folds them in for sleep.

She roams maternal hills and bright,
   Dark valleys safe and deep.
Into that tender breast at night
   The chastest stars may peep.
She walks—the lady of my delight—
   A shepherdess of sheep.

She holds her little thoughts in sight,
   Though gay they run and leap.
She is so circumspect and right;
   She has her soul to keep.
She walks—the lady of my delight—
   A shepherdess of sheep.

CHRIST IN THE UNIVERSE

By ALICE MEYNELL

With this ambiguous earth
His dealings have been told us. These abide:
The signal to a maid, the human birth,
The lesson, and the young Man crucified.

But not a star of all
The innumberable host of stars has heard
How He administered this terrestrial ball.
Our race have kept their Lord's entrusted Word.

Of His earth-visiting feet
None knows the secret, cherished, perilous,
The terrible, shamefast, frightened, whispered, sweet,
Heart-shattering secret of His way with us.

No planet knows that this
Our wayside planet, carrying land and wave,
Love and life multiplied, and pain and bliss,
Bears, as chief treasure, one forsaken grave,

Nor, in our little day,
May his devices with the heavens be guessed,
His pilgrimage to tread the Milky Way
Or His bestowals there be manifest.

But in the eternities,
Doubtless we shall compare together, hear
A million alien Gospels, in what guise
He trod the Pleiades, the Lyre, the Bear.

O, be prepared, my soul!
To read the inconceivable, to scan
The million forms of God those stars enroll
When, in our turn, we show to them a Man.

"I AM THE WAY"

By Alice Meynell

Thou art the Way.
Hadst Thou been nothing but the goal,
    I cannot say
If Thou hadst ever met my soul.

    I cannot see—
I, child of process—if there lies
    An end for me,
Full of repose, full of replies.

    I'll not reproach
The road that winds, my feet that err.
    Access, approach
Art Thou, Time, Way, and Wayfarer.

VIA, ET VERITAS, ET VITA

By Alice Meynell

"You never attained to Him." "If to attain
Be to abide, then that may be."
"Endless the way, followed with how much pain!"
"The way was He."

UNTO US A SON IS GIVEN

By ALICE MEYNELL

Given, not lent,
And not withdrawn—once sent,
This Infant of mankind, this One,
Is still the little welcome Son.

New every year,
New born and newly dear,
He comes with tidings and a song,
The ages long, the ages long;

Even as the cold
Keen winter grows not old,
As childhood is so fresh, foreseen,
And spring in the familiar green.

Sudden as sweet
Come the expected feet.
All joy is young, and new all art,
And He, too, Whom we have by heart.

TO A DAISY

By ALICE MEYNELL

Slight as thou art, thou art enough to hide
  Like all created things, secrets from me,
  And stand a barrier to eternity.
And I, how can I praise thee well and wide

From where I dwell—upon the hither side?
  Thou little veil for so great mystery,
  When shall I penetrate all things and thee,
And then look back? For this I must abide.

Till thou shalt grow and fold and be unfurled
Literally between me and the world.
  Then I shall drink from in beneath a spring.
And from a poet's side shall read his book.
O daisy mine, what will it be to look
  From God's side even of such a simple thing?

THE NEWER VAINGLORY

By ALICE MEYNELL

Two men went up to pray; and one gave thanks,
  Not with himself aloud,

With proclamation, calling on the ranks
    Of an attentive crowd.

"Thank God, I clap not my own humble breast,
    But other ruffians' backs,
Imputing crime—such is my tolerant haste—
    To any man that lacks.

"For I am tolerant, generous, keep no rules,
    And the age honors me.
Thank God, I am not as these rigid fools,
    Even as this Pharisee."

THE FOLDED FLOCK

By WILFRID MEYNELL

I saw the shepherd fold the sheep,
With all the little lambs that leap.
O Shepherd Lord, so I would be
Folded with all my family.
Or go they early, come they late,
Their mother and I must count them eight.
And how, for us, were any heaven
If we, sore-stricken, saw but seven?
Kind Shepherd, as of old Thou'lt run
And fold at need a straggling one.

CONVENT ECHOES

By HELEN LOUISE MORIARTY

Clear on the air, their pulsing cadence pealing,
   I hear a sweet refrain,
While o'er my thoughts a gentle mist is stealing,
   And mem'ries come again,

Of quiet halls where dusk is slow descending,
   Where peace has spread her wings.
Soft music in the distance only lending
   More charms where twilight clings.

Anon appear the black robed nuns, their faces
   Serene in sweet repose;
Across their brows the world has left no traces
   Of earthly dreams or woes.

Now loud on air the organ music swelling,
   They reach the chapel door—
The sweet faint incense stealing upward, telling
   'Tis Benediction's hour.

Now low-bowed heads, and hearts to Him ascending
   On incense laden air.
Ah surely Heaven must smile with ear attending
   The nun's low whispered prayer.

Fond memory lingers on those dim old hallways—
  Lingers and drops a tear,
And kind affection drapes the picture always
  Through each succeeding year.

ENGLAND

By JOHN HENRY NEWMAN

Tyre of the West, and glorying in the name
  More than in Faith's pure fame!
O trust not crafty fort nor rock renown'd
  Earn'd upon hostile ground;
Wielding Trade's master-keys, at thy proud will
To lock or loose its waters, England! trust not still.

Dread thine own power! Since haughty Babel's prime,
  High towers have been man's crime.
Since her hoar age, when the huge moat lay bare,
  Strongholds have been man's snare.
Thy nest is in the crags; ah, refuge frail!
Mad counsels in its hour, or traitors, will prevail.

He who scann'd Sodom for His righteous men
  Still spares thee for thy ten;
But, should vain tongues the Bride of Heaven defy,
  He will not pass thee by;

For, as earth's kings welcome their spotless guests,
So gives He them by turn, to suffer or be blest.

THE PILLAR OF THE CLOUD

By JOHN HENRY NEWMAN

Lead, Kindly Light, amid the encircling gloom,
    Lead Thou me on!
The night is dark, and I am far from home—
    Lead Thou me on!
Keep Thou my feet; I do not ask to see
The distant scene—one step enough for me.

I was not ever thus, nor pray'd that Thou
    Shouldst lead me on.
I lov'd to choose and see my path; but now
    Lead Thou me on!
I lov'd the garish day, and, spite of fears,
Pride rul'd my will: remember not past years.

So long Thy power hath bless'd me, sure it still
    Will lead me on,
O'er moor and fen, o'er crag and torrent, till
    The night is gone;
And with the morn those angel faces smile
Which I have lov'd long since, and lost awhile.

THE GREEK FATHERS

By JOHN HENRY NEWMAN

Let heathen sing thy heathen praise,
Fall'n Greece! the thought of holier days
    In my sad heart abides;
For sons of thine in Truth's first hour
Were tongues and weapons of His power,
Born of the Spirit's fiery shower,
    Our fathers and our guides.

All thine is Clement's varied page;
And Dionysius, ruler sage,
    In days of doubt and pain;
And Origen with eagle eye;
And saintly Basil's purpose high
    To smite imperial heresy,
And cleanse the Altar's stain.

From thee the glorious preacher came,
With soul of zeal and lips of flame,
    A court's stern martyr-guest;
And thine, O inexhaustive race!
Was Nazianzen's heaven-taught grace;
And royal hearted Athanase,
    With Paul's own mantel blessed.

RELICS OF SAINTS

By JOHN HENRY NEWMAN

"He is not the God of the dead, but of the living; for all live unto Him."

"The Fathers are in dust, yet live to God":
   So says the Truth; as if the motionless clay
Still held the seeds of life beneath the sod,
   Smouldering and straggling till the judgment day.

And hence we learn with reverence to esteem
   Of these frail houses, though the grave confines;
Sophist may urge his cunning tests, and deem
   That they are earth—but they are heavenly shrines.

THE SIGN OF THE CROSS

By JOHN HENRY NEWMAN

Whene'er across this sinful flesh of mine
   I draw the Holy Sign,
All good thoughts stir within me, and renew
   Their slumbering strength divine;
Till there springs up a courage high and true
   To suffer and to do.

And who shall say, but hateful spirits around,
  For their brief hour unbound,
Shudder to see, and wail their overthrow?
  While on far heathen ground
Some lonely Saint hails the fresh odour, though
  Its source he cannot know?

THE SON OF GOD

By CHARLES L. O'DONNELL, C.S.C.

The fount of Mary's joy
  Revealed now lies,
For, lo, has not the Boy
  His Father's eyes?

TO ST. JOSEPH

By CHARLES L. O'DONNELL, C.S.C.

St. Joseph, when the day was done
  And all your work put by,
You saw the stars come one by one
  Out in the violet sky.

You did not know the stars by name,
    But there sat at your knee
One who had made the light and flame
    And all things bright that be.

You heard with Him birds in the tree
    Twitter "Good-night" o'erhead—
The Maker of the world must see
    His little ones to bed.

Then when the darkness settled round,
    To Him your prayers were said;
No wonder that your sleep was ground
    The angels loved to tread.

THE DEAD MUSICIAN

By CHARLES L. O'DONNELL, C.S.C.

IN MEMORY OF BROTHER BASIL,
Organist for half a century at Notre Dame

He was the player and the played upon,
He was the actor and the acted on,
Artist, and yet himself a substance wrought;
God played on him as he upon the keys,
Moving his soul to mightiest melodies

Of lowly serving, hid austerities,
And holy thought that our high dream out-tops—
He was an organ where God kept the stops.
　　Naught, naught
Of all he gave us came so wondrous clear
As that he sounded to the Master's ear.

Wedded he was to the immortal Three,
Poverty, Obedience and Chastity,
And in a fourth he found them all expressed,
For him all gathered were in Music's breast,
　　And in God's house
　　He took her for his spouse—
High union that the world's eye never scans
　　Nor world's way knows.
Not any penny of applauding hands
He caught, nor would have caught,
　　Not any thought
　　Save to obey
Obedience that bade him play,
　　And for his bride
　　To have none else beside,
That both might keep unflecked their virgin snows.

Yet by our God's great law
Such marriage issue saw,
As they who cast away may keep,
　　Who sow not reap.
　　In Chastity entombed

His manhood bloomed,
And children not of earth
Had spotless birth.
With might unmortal was he strong
That he begot
Of what was not,
Within the barren womb of silence, song.
Yea, many sons he had
To make his sole heart glad—
Romping the boundless meadows of the air,
Skipping the cloudy hills, and climbing bold
The heavens' nightly stairs of starry gold.
Nay, winning heaven's door
To mingle evermore
With deathless troops of angel harmony.
He filled the house of God
With servants at his nod,
A music-host of moving pagentry.
Lo, this priest, and that an acolyte:
Ah, such we name aright
Creative art,
To body forth love slumbering at the heart…
Fools, they who pity him,
Imagine dim
Days that the world's glare brightens not.
Until the seraphim
Shake from their flashing hair
Lightnings, and weave serpents there,
His days we reckon fair.…

Yet more he had than this;
Lord of the liberative kiss,
To own and yet refrain,
To hold his hand in reign.
High continence of his high power,
That turns from virtue's very flower,
In loss of that elected pain
A greater prize to gain.
As one who long had put wine by
Would now himself deny
Water, and thirsting die.
So, sometimes he was idle at the keys,
Pale fingers on the aged ivories;
Then, like a prisoned bird,
Music was seen, not heard,
Then were his quivering hands most strong
With blood of the repressed song—
A fruitful barrenness. Oh, where
Out of angelic air,
This side the heavens' spheres
Such sight to start and hinder tears.
Who knows, perhaps while silence throbbed
He heard the De Profundis sobbed
By his own organ at his bier today—
It is the saints' anticipative way,
He knew both hand and ear were clay.
That was one thought
Never is music wrought,
For silence only could that truth convey.

Widowed of him, his organ now is still,
His music-children fled, their echoing feet yet fill
The blue, far reaches of the vaulted nave,
The heart that sired them, pulseless in the grave.
Only the song he made is hushed, his soul,
Responsive to God's touch, in His control
Elsewhere shall tune the termless ecstasy
　　Of one who all his life kept here
　　　　An alien ear,
Homesick for harpings of eternity.

GIOTTO'S CAMPANILE

By THOMAS O'HAGAN

O pulsing heart with voice attuned
　　To all the soul builds high,
Framing in notes of love divine
　　A drama of the sky,
Across the Arno's flowing tide
　　The notes chime on the air,
Deep as the mysteries of God
　　And tender as a prayer.

Here, where the Poet of Sorrows dwelt,
　　Whose altar Love had built,
And framed his morn in dreams so pure

That knew not stain nor guilt:
O Vita Nuova! Earthly Love
    Then changed to love Divine;
Transfigured at the wedding-feast,
    Earth's grapes are heavenly wine.

Where cowled monk with soul of fire
    Struck vice athwart the face,
With God's anointed sword of truth
    That flashed with beams of grace.
O bitter days of war and strife!
    Heaven's ardor was too great;
The Empire of the earth held sway
    And sealed with saddest fate.

Methinks I hear from thy strong lips,
    O century-dowered bell!
The story of the Whites and Blacks,
    As banners rose or fell;
Methinks I hear an epic voice,
    Full of God's love and power,
With accent of an Exile sad
    Speaking from out thy tower!

NAME OF MARY

By JOHN BOYLE O'REILLY

Dear, honored name, beloved for human ties,
   But loved and honored first that One was given
In living proof, to erring mortal eyes,
   That our poor flesh is near akin to heaven.

Sweet word of dual meaning: one of grace,
   And born of our kind Advocate above;
And one, by mercy linked to that dear face
   That blessed my childhood with its mother-love,

And taught me first the simple prayer: "To thee,
   Poor banished sons of Eve, we send our cries."
Through mist of years, those words recall to me
   A childish face upturned to loving eyes.

And yet, to some the name of Mary bears
   No special meaning and no gracious power;
In that dear word they seek for hidden snares,
   As wasps find poison in the sweetest flower.

But faithful hearts can see, o'er doubts and fears,
   The Virgin-link that binds the Lord to earth;
Which, to the upturned trusting face, appears
   Greater than angel, though of human birth.

The sweet-faced moon reflects, on cheerless night,
  The rays of hidden sun that rise tomorrow;
So, unseen God still lets his promised light,
  Through holy Mary, shine upon our sorrow.

A CHRISTMAS CAROL

By MARY A. O'REILLY

Night in the far Judean land,
  The pregnant air is still,
The sky one blue unclouded band,
  Seems drooping o'er each hill.
The hills then toward each other bend,
Some mighty secret to portend.
  Gloria in excelsis Deo.

The sheep in near-by pastures browse,
  Some bleat as if in pain;
The youthful shepherds watch and drowse,
  Then drowse and watch again;
When lo! a light from Heaven appears
Which makes them huddle in their fears.
  Gloria in excelsis Deo.

God's glory shone around them there,
  And then an angel cried—

"Fear not, for I good tidings bear
   To you, and all beside.
For unto you is born this day
A Savior, Christ the Lord." We pray—
   Gloria in excelsis Deo.

Then swinging from the skies there came
   Groups of the heavenly host,
Praising the Lord in sweet acclaim—
   The burden of their toast—
"Glory to God on High," again—
His "Peace on earth, good will to men."
   Gloria in excelsis Deo.

Within a stable sweet with hay,
   And warm with breath of kine,
The Baby and His Mother lay,
   O, mystery divine!
The bed of straw a cloud appears,
We hear the music of the spheres.
   Gloria in excelsis Deo.

Dear maiden mother, let us now,
   While to your breast He clings,
In humble adoration bow
   With shepherds and with kings,
And at His feet our off'ring be
Praise, love, faith, hope and charity.
   Gloria in excelsis Deo.

ROMA MATER SEMPAETERNA

By SHAEMAS O. SHEEL

The blue skies bend and are about her furled,
   A maiden mantle; and with lilies bright
   The sun daywhiles doth crown her, and at night
With stars her garment's border is empearled.
Not a king's favorite, perfumed and curled,
     Is half so fair; no queen of martial might
   So potent as the Mother of the Light,
The Mary of the Cities of the World!

Eternal Mother, at whose breasts of white
   The infant Church was suckled and made strong
     With the sweet milk of heavenly Truth and Love,
     O thou that art all nations set above,
   Strengthen us still because the way is long,
Mary of Cities, Mother of the Light!

MARY'S BABY

By SHAEMAS O. SHEEL

Joseph, mild and noble, bent above the straw:
A pale girl, a frail girl, suffering, he saw;
"O my Love, my Mary, my bride, I pity thee!"

"Nay, Dear," said Mary, "All is well with me!"
"Baby, my Baby, O my Babe," she sang.
Suddenly the golden night all with music rang.

Angels leading shepherds, shepherds leading sheep:
The silence of worship broke the mother's sleep.
All the meek and lowly of the world were there;
Smiling she showed them that her Child was fair.
"Baby, my Baby," kissing Him she said.
Suddenly a flaming star through the heavens sped.

Three old men and weary knelt them side by side,
The world's wealth forswearing, majesty and pride;
Worldly might and wisdom before the Babe bent low:
Weeping, maid Mary said "I love Him so!"
"Baby, my Baby," and the Baby slept.
Suddenly on Calvary all the olives wept.

THEY WENT FORTH TO BATTLE

By SHAEMAS O. SHEEL

They went forth to battle, but they always fell;
Their eyes were fixed above the sullen shields;
Nobly they fought and bravely, but not well,
And sank heart-wounded by a subtle spell.
They knew not fear that to the foeman yields,

They were not weak, as one who vainly wields
A futile weapon, yet the sad scrolls tell
How on the hard-fought field they always fell.

It was a secret music that they heard,
    A sad sweet plea for pity and for peace;
And that which pierced the heart was but a word,
Though the white breast was red-lipped where the sword
        Pressed a fierce cruel kiss, to put surcease
        On its hot thirst, but drank a hot increase.
Ah, then by some strange troubling doubt were stirred,
And died for hearing what no foeman heard.

They went forth to battle but they always fell;
    Their might was not the might of lifted spears;
Over the battle-clamor came a spell
Of troubling music, and they fought not well.
        Their wreaths are willows and their tribute, tears;
        Their names are old sad stories in men's ears;
Yet they will scatter the red hordes of Hell,
Who went to battle forth and always fell.

HE WHOM A DREAM HATH POSSESSED

By SHAEMAS O. SHEEL

He whom a dream hath possessed knoweth no more of
doubting,
For mist and the blowing of winds and the mouthing of words
he scorns;
Not the sinuous speech of schools he hears, but a knightly
shouting,
And never comes darkness down, yet he greeteth a million
morns.
He whom a dream hath possessed knoweth no more of
roaming;
All roads and the flowing of waves and the speediest flight he
knows,
But wherever his feet are set, his soul is forever homing,
And going he comes, and coming he heareth a call and goes.
He whom a dream hath possessed knoweth no more of sorrow,
At death and the dropping of leaves and the fading of suns he
smiles,
For a dream remembers no past and scorns the desire of a
morrow,
And a dream in a sea of doom sets surely the ultimate isles.
He whom a dream hath possessed treads the impalpable
marches,
From the dust of the day's long road he leaps to a laughing star,
And the ruin of worlds that fall he views from eternal arches,
And rides God's battle-field in a flashing and golden car.

MARIA IMMACULATA

By CONDÉ BENOIST PALLEN

I.

How may I sing, unworthy I,
Our Lady's glorious sanctity?
She whose celestial shoon
Rest on the horned moon
In Heaven's highest galaxy;
She whom the poet sang of old
In that rare vision told
In soft Tuscan speech of gold,
The spotless spouse and mother-maid
The goodliest sapphire in Heaven's floor inlaid,
Around whom wheels the circling flame
Of the rapt seraph breathing Mary's name,
While choir to choir replies
In growing harmonies
Through all the glowing spheres of Paradise,
Till universal Heaven's glad estate
Rings jubilation to their queen immaculate.

II.

Ah me! Unworthy I to sing
The stainless mother of my King,
My King and Lord,
The Incarnate Word,
Heaven itself comprest

Within her virgin breast!
How may my faltering rhyme
Sing of Eternity in time,
Omnipotence in human frailty exprest,
Our earthly garden fragrant with celestial thyme.
What Muse, though great Urania guide her flight,
May dare the sacrosanct and awful height
Of that mysterious sublime
Within the secret counsels of the Infinite!
Omniscence there supreme and sole
Clasps the beginning and the whole
Of Love beyond created sight,
Uncreate and quintessential light!
Before the splendor of that ray
Cherub and seraph fall away
Dazzled and broken by excess
Of everpowering blessedness,
Yet panting for the fulness of the bliss
That breathes consuming fire from Love's unkenned abyss.
Not through that fiery sphere my way,
But here where shines the veiléd day,
The flames of mystery insteeped
In this our mortal clay;
For in her maiden breast asleep
Lies all the Love of Heaven's deep,
The holy circle of her zone
Incarnate Love's terrestrial throne.

III.

The great archangel veils his face
Before her: "Hail, full of grace!"
And Heaven is clasped of earth;
While all the wheeling spheres with all their choirs
Around her wheel seraphic fires.
Eden rises to its second birth;
Again the prime estate
Of man is renovate,
And all the elder worth renewed in her immaculate;
Virgin and spouse of Him
Who breathes the virtue of the Seraphim,
Virgin and mother of the Eternal Son,
Daughter, Virgin, Spouse in one!
The spotless mate of spotless Dove,
The one great miracle of God's love,
From all eternity the chosen bride,
Save only her none, none
Exempt from sin's dominion;
Save only her of Adam's race
Or heavenly line, none full of grace;
On her alone, on her alone
The torrent of His love poured down
The deep abundance of its flood
Into the pure channels of her maidenhood,
The fleckless mirror of her grace
Reflecting all the beauty of His Face.

IV.

She looks with human eyes
Into the eyes of Paradise;
Upon her virgin breast the Babe Divine
Gazes again into her eyne;
O vanity of words to tell
The wonder of that spell,
The ravishment of bliss
Upwelling from the deep abyss
Of Love incarnate gazing in the eyes
Of his terrestrial paradise!
See Heaven within her arms,
Gathered against all harms,
Innocence by innocence addrest,
Virgin love by virgin love carest,
The sinless mother and the sinless Son
For Heaven and earth to gaze upon!
Her living image on her knee,
O the depths of her maternity!
Her God, her Infant at her breast,
O Love beyond all utterance exprest,
The Eternal Word in virgin flesh made manifest!

V.

Ye sons of Adam rejoice
With exultant voice!
Shake off your chains! Arise!
The ancient dragon has no power
O'er Jesse's virgin flower,

And stricken 'neath a maiden's sandal lies.
Nor may his venomed breath so much
As her garment's outer margin touch;
And sin's torrential flood,
That whelmed all Adam's flesh and blood,
Its loathsome stream turns back
Before her footsteps' radiant track.

VI.

Rejoice, children of men!
Behold again
Your flesh rejuvenate
In her immaculate!
Rejoice with exceeding joy,
For in her free from sin's alloy
Your renovated race
In plentitude of grace
Dare look again unshamed upon its Maker's Face!
Chosen to bear the Eternal Word,
In her your more than dignity restored;
In her the more than golden worth
Of Eden's prime when Heaven was linked with earth;
Unstained by Adam's guilty forfeiture,
In her your long corrupted flesh made pure;
For of her, flesh of flesh and bone of bone,
Eternal Love builds up His stainless throne!

VII.

Rejoice and be glad this day!

In jubilation lay

Your tribute at her feet,

Spotless and most meet,

The mystic rose of Jesse's root,

To bear the heavenly fruit;

Wisdom's seat and Heaven's gate,

Our surest advocate,

Mother of God immaculate!

Be glad, O Adam's clay,

Be glad this happy day.

And with accordant voice acclaim

Our spotless Lady's stainless fame;

Be ye exceeding glad and sing

The mother of our King.

And though unworthy be my strain,

She is too tender not to deign

To lend a gracious ear

To this her children's humble prayer:

Mother of Mercy, hear!

Mother whose face is likest His,

Who our Redeemer is,

Grant us one day to share

Thy happiness in gazing on His Face,

Who found thee without spot and full of grace!

THE RAISING OF THE FLAG

By CONDÉ BENOIST PALLEN

Lift up the banner of our love
To the kiss of the winds above,
The banner of the world's fair hope,
Set with stars from the azure cope,
When liberty was young,
And yet unsung
Clarioned her voice among
The trodden peoples, and stirred
The pulses with her word,
Till the swift flood red
From the quick heart sped,
Flushing valour's cheek with flame
At sounding of her august sacred name!

Lift up the banner of the stars,
The standard of the double bars,
Red with the holy tide
Of heroes' blood, who died
At the feet of liberty,
Shouting her battle-cry
Triumphantly
As they fell like sickled corn
In that first resplendent morn
Of freedom, glad to die
In the dawn of her clear eye!

Lift up the flag of starry blue
Caught from the crystal hue
Of central heaven's glowing dome,
Where the great winds largely roam
In unrestrainéd liberty;
Caught from the cerulean sea
Of midmost ocean tossing free,
Flecked with the racing foam
Of rushing waters, as they leap
Unbridled from the laughing deep
In the gulfs of liberty!

Lift up the banner red
With the blood of heroes shed
In victory!
Lift up the banner blue
As heaven, and as true
In constancy!
Lift up the banner white
As sea foam in the light
Of liberty;
The banner of the triple hue,
The banner of the red and white and blue,
Bright ensign of the free!

Lift up the banner of the days to come,
When cease the trumpet and the rolling drum;
When peace in the nest of love
Unfolds the wings of the dove,

Brooding o'er the days to be,
Peace born of freedom's might,
Peace sprung from the power of right,
The peace of liberty!

Lift up the flag of high surprise
To greet the gladdened eyes
Of peoples far and near,
The glorious harbinger
Of earth's wide liberties,
Streaming pure and clear
In freedom's lofty atmosphere!

Lift up our hearts to Him who made to shine
In Heaven's arch the glorious sign
Of mercy's heavenly birth
To all the peoples of the earth,
The pledge of peace divine!
And let our glorious banner, too,
The banner of the rainbow's hue,
In heaven's wide expanse unfurled,
Be for a promise to the world
Of peace to all mankind;
Banner of peace and light,
Banner of red and blue and white,
Red as the crimson blood
Of Christ's wide brotherhood,
Blue with the unchanging hope
Of heaven's steadfast sun,

White as the radiant sun
The whole earth shining on!

THE BABE OF BETHLEHEM

By CONDÉ BENOIST PALLEN

O cruel manger, how bleak, how bleak!
  For the limbs of the Babe, my God;
Soft little limbs on the cold, cold straw;
  Weep, O eyes, for thy God!

Bitter ye winds in the frosty night
  Upon the Babe, my God,
Piercing the torn and broken thatch;
  Lament, O heart, for thy God!

Bare is the floor, how bare, how bare
  For the Babe's sweet mother, my God;
Only a stable for mother and Babe;
  How cruel thy world, my God!

Cast out, cast out, by his brother men
  Unknown the Babe, my God;
The ox and the ass alone are there;
  Soften, O heart, for thy God!

Dear little arms and sweet little hands,
   That stretch for thy mother, my God;
Soft baby eyes to the mother's eyes;
   Melt, O heart, for thy God!

Waxen touches on mother's heart,
   Fingers of the Babe, my God;
Dear baby lips to her virgin breast,
   The virgin mother of God.

The shepherds have come from the hills to adore
   The Babe in the manger, my God;
Mary and Joseph welcome them there;
   Worship, O soul, thy God!

But I alone may not come near
   The Babe in the manger, my God;
Weep for thy sins, O heart, and plead
   With Mary the mother of God.

May I not come, oh, just to the door,
   To see the Babe, my God;
There will I stop and kneel and adore,
   And weep for my sins, O God!

But Mary smiles, and rising up,
   In her arms the Babe, my God,
She comes to the door and bends her down,
   With the Babe in her arms, my God!

Her sinless arms in my sinful arms
  Place the Babe, my God;
"He has come to take thy sins away";
  Break, O heart, for thy God!

THE TOYS

By COVENTRY PATMORE

My little son, who look'd from thoughtful eyes
And mov'd and spoke in quiet grown-up wise,
Having my law the seventh time disobey'd,
I struck him, and dismiss'd
With hard words and unkiss'd,
His Mother, who was patient, being dead.
Then fearing lest his grief should hinder him sleep
I visited his bed,
But found him slumbering deep,
With darken'd eyelids, and their lashes yet
From his late sobbing wet.
And I, with moan,
Kissing away his tears, left others of my own;
For, on a table drawn beside his head,
He had put, within his reach,
A box of counters and a red-vein'd stone,
A piece of glass abraded by the beach,
And six or seven shells,

A bottle with bluebells
And two French copper coins, ranged there with careful art,
To comfort his sad heart.
So when that night I pray'd
To God, I wept, and said:
Ah, when at last we lie with trancéd breath,
Not vexing Thee in death,
And Thou rememberest of what toys
We made our joys,
How weakly understood
Thy great commanded good,
Then, fatherly not less
Than I whom Thou hast moulded from the clay,
Thou'lt leave Thy wrath, and say,
"I will be sorry for their childishness."

"IF I WERE DEAD"

By COVENTRY PATMORE

"If I were dead, you'd some time say, Poor Child!"
The dear lips quiver'd as they spake,
And the tears break
From eyes, which, not to grieve me, brightly smiled.
Poor Child, poor Child!
I seem to hear your laugh, your talk, your song.
It is not true that Love will do no wrong.

Poor Child!
And did you think, when you so cried and smiled,
How I, in lonely nights, should lie awake,
And of those words your full avengers make?
Poor Child, poor Child!
And now, unless it be
That sweet amends thrice told are come to thee,
O God, have Thou no mercy upon me!
Poor Child!

DEPARTURE

By COVENTRY PATMORE

It was not like your great and gracious ways!
Do you, that have nought other to lament,
Never, my Love, repent
Of how, that July afternoon,
You went,
With sudden, unintelligible phrase,
And frightened eye,
Upon your journey of so many days
Without a single kiss, or a good-bye?
I knew, indeed, that you were parting soon;
And so we sate, within the low sun's rays,
You whispering to me, for your voice was weak,
Your harrowing praise.

Well, it was well
To hear you such things speak,
And I could tell
What made your eyes a growing gloom of love,
As a warm South-wind sombres a March grove.
And it was like your great and gracious ways
To turn your talk on daily things, my Dear,
Lifting the luminous, pathetic lash
To let the laughter flash,
Whilst I drew near,
Because you spoke so low that I could scarcely hear.
But all at once to leave me at the last,
More at the wonder than the loss aghast,
With huddled, unintelligible phrase,
And frighten'd eye,
And go your journey of all days
With not one kiss, or a good-bye,
And the only loveless look the look with which you passed;
'Twas all unlike your great and gracious ways.

REGINA CAELI

By COVENTRY PATMORE

Say, did his sisters wonder what could Joseph see
In a mild, silent little Maid like thee?
And was it awful, in that narrow house,

With God for Babe and Spouse?
Nay, like thy simple, female sort, each one
Apt to find Him in Husband and in Son,
Nothing to thee came strange in this.
Thy wonder was but wondrous bliss:
Wondrous, for, though
True Virgin lives not but does know,
(Howbeit none ever yet confess'd)
That God lies really in her breast,
Of thine He made His special nest!
And so
All mothers worship little feet,
And kiss the very ground they've trod;
But, ah, thy little Baby sweet
Who was indeed thy God!

IDEAL

By P. H. PEARSE
(*Translated from the Irish by Thomas MacDonagh.*)

Naked I saw thee,
  O beauty of beauty!
And I blinded my eyes
  For fear I should flinch.
I heard thy music,
  O sweetness of sweetness!

And I shut my ears
  For fear I should fail.
I kissed thy lips,
  O sweetness of sweetness!
And I hardened my heart
  For fear of my ruin.
I blinded my eyes,
  And my ears I shut,
I hardened my heart
  And my love I quenched.
I turned my back
  On the dream I had shaped,
And to this road before me
  My face I turned.
I set my face
  To the road here before me,
To the work that I see,
  To the death that I shall meet.

MUSIC

By CHARLES PHILLIPS

There is a hunger in my heart tonight,
  A longing in my soul, to hear
The voice of heaven o'er the noise of earth
  That doth assail mine ear.

For we are exiled children of the skies,
    Lone and lost wanderers from home...
The stars come out like lamps in windows lit
    Far, far from where we roam;
Like candles lit to show the long late way,
    Dear kindly beacons sure and bright;
But O, the heavy journeying, and O
    The silence of the night!—
The dark and vasty silences that lie
    Between the going and the goal!
Will not God reach a friendly hand to lift
    And land my weary soul?
Will not God speak a friendly word to me
    Above the tumult and the din
Of earthly things—one little word to hush
    The voice of care and sin? ...
He speaks! He answers my poor faltering prayer!
    He opens heaven's lattice wide;
He bids me bathe my brow in heavenly airs
    Like to a flowing tide!
He calls; He gives unto my famished soul,
    Unto my eager heart, its meed:
He breathes upon me with the breath of song,
    And O, my soul is freed,
And I am lifted up and up, and held
    A little while—a child, to see
The beauties of my Father's house, which shall
    No more be shut from me!

I SEE HIS BLOOD UPON THE ROSE

By JOSEPH MARY PLUNKETT

I see His blood upon the rose
  And in the stars the glory of His eyes,
His Body gleams amid eternal snows,
  His tears fall from the skies.

I see His face in every flower;
  The thunder and the singing of the birds
Are but His voice—and carven by His power
  Rocks are His written words.

All pathways by His feet are worn,
  His strong heart stirs the ever-beating sea,
His crown of thorns is twined with every thorn,
  His cross is every tree.

THE STARS SANG IN GOD'S GARDEN

By JOSEPH MARY PLUNKETT

The stars sang in God's garden;
The stars are the birds of God;
The night-time is God's harvest,
Its fruits are the words of God.

God ploughed His fields at morning,
God sowed His seed at noon,
God reaped and gathered in His corn
With the rising of the moon.

The sun rose up at midnight,
The sun rose red as blood,
It showed the Reaper, the dead Christ,
Upon His cross of wood.

For many live that one may die,
And one must die that many live—
The stars are silent in the sky
Lest my poor songs be fugitive.

"IS IT NOTHING TO YOU?"

By MAY PROBYN

We were playing on the green together,
  My sweetheart and I—
Oh, so heedless in the gay June weather,
  When the word went forth that we must die.
Oh, so merrily the balls of amber
  And of ivory tossed we to the sky,
While the word went forth in the King's chamber,
  That we both must die.

Oh, so idly, straying through the pleasaunce,
    Plucked we here and there
Fruit and bud, while in the royal presence
    The King's son was casting from his hair
Glory of the wreathen gold that crowned it,
    And, ungirding all his garment fair,
Flinging by the jewelled clasp that bound it,
    With his feet made bare,

Down the myrtled stairway of the palace,
    Ashes on his head,
Came he, through the rose and citron alleys,
    In the rough sark of sackcloth habited,
And in a hempen halter—oh! we jested,
    Lightly, and we laughed as he was led
To the torture, while the bloom we breasted
    Where the grapes grew red.

Oh, so sweet the birds, when he was dying,
    Piped to her and me—
Is no room this glad June day for sighing—
    He is dead, and she and I go free!
When the sun shall set on all our pleasure
    We will mourn him—What, so you decree
We are heartless?—Nay, but in what measure
    Do you more than we?

THE BEES OF MYDDLETON MANOR
17TH CENTURY

By MAY PROBYN

Buzzing, buzzing, buzzing, my golden-belted bees:
My little son was seven years old—the mint-flower
  touched his knees;
Yellow were his curly locks;
Yellow were his stocking-clocks;
His plaything of a sword had a diamond in its hilt;
Where the garden beds lay sunny,
And the bees were making honey,
"For God and the king—to arms! to arms!" the day long
  would he lilt.
Smock'd in lace and flowered brocade, my pretty son of seven
Wept sore because the kitten died, and left the charge uneven.
"I head one battalion, mother—
Kitty," sobbed he, "led the other!
And when we reach'd the bee-hive bench
We used to halt and storm the trench:
If we could plant our standard here,
With all the bees a-buzzing near,
And fly the colors safe from sting,
The town was taken for the king!"
Flirting flitting over the thyme, by bees with yellow band—
My little son of seven came close, and clipp'd me by the hand;
A wreath of mourning cloth was wound
His small left arm and sword-hilt round,

And on the thatch of every hive a whisp of black was bound.

"Sweet mother, we must tell the bees, or they will swarm away:

Ye little bees!" he called, "draw nigh, and hark to what I say,

And make us golden honey still for our white wheaten bread,

> Though never more
> We rush on war
> With Kitty at our head:
> Who'll give the toast
> When swords are cross'd,
> Now Kitty lieth dead?"

Buzzing, buzzing, buzzing, my bees of yellow girth:

My son of seven changed his mood, and clasp'd me in his mirth.

"Sweet mother, when I grow a man and fall on battlefield,"

He cried, and down in the daisied grass upon one knee he kneel'd,

"I charge thee, come and tell the bees how I for the king lie dead;

And thou shalt never lack fine honey for thy wheaten bread!"

Flitting, flitting, flitting, my busy bees, alas!

No footsteps of my soldier son came clinking through the grass.

> Thrice he kiss'd me for farewell;
> And far on the stone his shadow fell;

He buckled spurs and sword-belt on, as the sun began to stoop,

Set foot in stirrup, and sprang to horse, and rode to join his troop.

To the west he rode, where the winds were at play,
And Monmouth's army mustering lay;
Where Bridgewater flew her banner high,
And gave up her keys, when the Duke came by;
And the maids of Taunton paid him court
With colors their own white hands had wrought;
And red as a field, where blood doth run,
Sedgemoor blazed in the setting sun.

Broider'd sash and clasp of gold, my soldier son, alas!
The mint was all in flower, and the clover in the grass:
    "With every bed
    In bloom," I said,
  "What further lack the bees,
    That they buzz so loud,
    Like a restless cloud,
  Among the orchard trees?"
No voice in the air, from Sedgemoor field,
Moan'd out how Grey and the horse had reel'd;
Met me no ghost, with haunting eyes,
That westward pointed 'mid its sighs,
And pull'd apart a bloody vest,
And show'd the sword-gash in his breast.

Empty hives, and flitting bees, and sunny morning hours;
I snipp'd the blossom'd lavender, and the pinks, and the
    gillyflowers;
        No petal trembled in my hold—
        I saw not the dead stretched stark and cold

On the trampled turf at the shepherd's door,
In the cloak and the doublet Monmouth wore,
With Monmouth's scarf and headgear on,
And the eyes, not clos'd, of my soldier son;
I knew not how, ere the cocks did crow, the fight was fought
in the dark,
With naught for guide but the enemy's guns, when the flint
flash'd out a spark,
Till, routed at first sound of fire, the cavalry broke and fled,
And the hoofs struck dumb, where they spurn'd the slain, and
the meadow stream ran red;
I saw not the handful of horsemen spur through the dusk,
and out of sight,
My soldier son at the Duke's left hand, and Grey that rode on
his right.
Buzzing, buzzing, buzzing, my honey-making bees,
They left the musk, and the marigolds and the scented faint
sweet peas;
They gather'd in a darkening cloud, and sway'd, and rose to fly;
A blackness on the summer blue, they swept across the sky.
Gaunt and ghastly with gaping wounds—(my soldier son,
alas!)
Footsore and faint, the messenger came halting through the
grass.
The wind went by and shook the leaves—the mint-stalk shed
its flower—
And I miss'd the murmuring round the hives, and my boding
heart beat slower.
    His soul we cheer'd with meat and wine;

With woman's craft and balsam fine
We bathed his hurts, and bound them soft,
While west the wind played through the croft,
And the low sun dyed the pinks blood red,
And, straying near the mint-flower shed,
A wild bee wantoned o'er the bed.

He told how my son, at the shepherd's door, kept watch in
  Monmouth's clothes,
While Monmouth donned the shepherd's frock, in hope to
  cheat his foes.
     A couple of troopers spied him stand,
     And bade him yield to the king's command:
     "Surrender, thou rebel as good as dead,
     A price is set on thy traitor head!"
     My soldier son, with secret smile,
     Held both at bay for a little while,
     Dealt them such death blow as he fell,
     Neither was left the tale to tell;
     With dying eyes that asked no grace,
     They stared on him for a minute's space,
     And felt that it was not Monmouth's face.
Crimsoned through was Monmouth's cloak, when the soldier
  dropped at their side—
"Those knaves will carry no word," he said, and he smiled in
  his pain, and died.
"Two days," told the messenger, "did we lie
     Hid in the fields of peas and rye,
     Hid in the ditch of brake and sedge,

With the enemy's scouts down every hedge,
Till Grey was seized, and Monmouth seized, that under the
    fern did crouch,
Starved and haggard, and all unshaved, with a few raw peas
    in his pouch."

No music soundeth in my ears, but a passing bell that tolls
For gallant lords with head on block—sweet Heaven receive
    their souls!
    And a mound, unnamed, in Sedgemoor grass,
    That laps my soldier son, alas!
        The bloom is shed—
        The bees are fled—
Middleton luck it's done and dead.

A LEGEND

By ADELAIDE ANNE PROCTER

I.

The Monk was preaching: strong his earnest word,
From the abundance of his heart he spoke,
And the flame spread—in every soul that heard
Sorrow and love and good resolve awoke
The poor lay Brother, ignorant and old,
Thanked God that he had heard such words of gold.

II.

"Still let the glory, Lord, be thine alone,"—
So prayed the Monk, his heart absorbed in praise:
"Thine be the glory: if my hands have sown
The harvest ripened in Thy mercy's rays,
It was Thy blessing, Lord, that made my word
Bring light and love to every soul that heard."

III.

"O Lord, I thank Thee that my feeble strength
Has been so blest; that sinful hearts and cold
Were melted at my pleading—knew at length
How sweet Thy service and how safe Thy fold:
While souls that loved Thee saw before them rise
Still holier heights of loving sacrifice."

IV.

So prayed the Monk: when suddenly he heard
An Angel speaking thus: "Know, O my Son,
The words had all been vain, but hearts were stirred,
And saints were edified, and sinners won,
By his, the poor lay Brother's humble aid
Who sat upon the pulpit stair and prayed."

THE SACRED HEART

By ADELAIDE ANNE PROCTER

What wouldst thou have, O soul,
  Thou weary soul?
Lo! I have sought for rest
On the Earth's heaving breast,
  From pole to pole.
Sleep—I have been with her,
  But she gave dreams;
Death—nay, the rest he gives
  Rest only seems.
Fair nature knows it not—
  The grass is growing;
The blue air knows it not—
  The winds are blowing:
Not in the changing sky,
  The stormy sea,
Yet somewhere in God's wide world
  Rest there must be.
Within thy Saviour's Heart
  Place all thy care,
And learn, O weary soul,
  Thy Rest is there.

What wouldst thou, trembling soul?
  Strength for the strife—
Strength for this fiery war

That we call Life.
Fears gather thickly round;
  Shadowy foes,
Like unto armed men,
  Around me close.
What am I, frail and poor,
  When griefs arise?
No help from the weak earth,
  Or the cold skies.
Lo! I can find no guards,
  No weapons borrow;
Shrinking, alone I stand,
  With mighty sorrow.
Courage, thou trembling soul,
  Grief thou must bear,
Yet thou canst find a strength
  Will match despair;
Within thy Saviour's Heart—
  Seek for it there.

What wouldst thou have, sad soul,
  Oppressed with grief?—
Comfort: I seek in vain,
  Nor find relief.
Nature, all pitiless,
  Smiles on my pain;
I ask my fellow-men,
  They give disdain.
I asked the babbling streams,

But they flowed on;
I asked the wise and good,
  But they gave none.
Though I have asked the stars,
  Coldly they shine.
They are too bright to know
  Grief such as mine.
I asked for comfort still,
  And I found tears,
And I have sought in vain
  Long, weary years.
Listen, thou mournful soul,
  Thy pain shall cease;
Deep in His sacred Heart
  Dwells joy and peace.

Yes, in that Heart divine
  The Angels bright
Find, through eternal years,
  Still new delight.
From thence his constancy
  The martyr drew,
And there the virgin band
  Their refuge knew.
There, racked by pain without,
  And dread within,
How many souls have found
  Heaven's bliss begin.
Then leave thy vain attempts

To seek for peace;
The world can never give
One soul release;
But in thy Saviour's Heart
Securely dwell,
No pain can harm thee, hid
In that sweet cell.
Then fly, O coward soul,
Delay no more:
What words can speak the joy
For thee in store?
What smiles of earth can tell
Of peace like thine?
Silence and tears are best
For things divine.

THE ANNUNCIATION

By ADELAIDE ANNE PROCTER

How pure, and frail, and white,
The snowdrops shine!
Gather a garland bright
For Mary's shrine.
For, born of winter snows,
These fragile flowers
Are gifts to our fair Queen

From Spring's first hours.
For on this blessèd day
    She knelt at prayer;
When, lo! before her shone
    An Angel fair.
"Hail, Mary!" thus he cried,
    With reverent fear:
She, with sweet wondering eyes,
    Marvelled to hear.
Be still, ye clouds of Heaven!
    Be silent, Earth!
And hear an Angel tell
    Of Jesus' birth,
While she, whom Gabriel hails
    As full of grace,
Listens with humble faith
    In her sweet face.
Be still—Pride, War, and Pomp,
    Vain Hopes, vain Fears,
For now an Angel speaks,
    And Mary hears.
"Hail, Mary!" lo, it rings
    Through ages on;
"Hail Mary!" it shall sound,
    Till Time is done
"Hail, Mary!" infant lips
    Lisp it today;
"Hail, Mary!" with faint smile
    The dying say.

"Hail, Mary!" many a heart
  Broken with grief,
In that angelic prayer
  Has found relief.
And many a half-lost soul,
  When turned at bay,
With those triumphant words
  Has won the day.
"Hail, Mary, Queen of Heaven!"
  Let us repeat,
And place our snowdrop wreath
  Here at her feet.

OUR DAILY BREAD

By ADELAIDE ANNE PROCTER

Give us our daily Bread,
  O God, the bread of strength!
For we have learnt to know
  How weak we are at length.
As children we are weak,
  As children must be fed—
Give us Thy Grace, O Lord,
  To be our daily Bread.
Give us our daily Bread—
  The bitter bread of grief.

We sought earth's poisoned feasts
  For pleasure and relief;
We sought her deadly fruits,
  But now, O God, instead,
We ask thy healing grief
  To be our daily Bread.

Give us our daily Bread
  To cheer our fainting soul;
The feast of comfort, Lord,
  And peace, to make us whole:
For we are sick of tears,
  The useless tears we shed;
Now give us comfort, Lord,
  To be our daily Bread.
Give us our daily Bread,
  The Bread of Angels, Lord,
For us, so many times,
  Broken, betrayed, adored:
His Body and His Blood;
  The feast that Jesus spread:
Give Him—our life, our all—
  To be our daily Bread!

MY MARYLAND

By JAMES RYDER RANDALL

The despot's heel is on thy shore,
    Maryland!
His torch is at thy temple door,
    Maryland!
Avenge the patriotic gore
That flecked the streets of Baltimore,
And be the battle-queen of yore,
    Maryland, my Maryland!
Hark to an exiled son's appeal,
    Maryland!
My Mother State, to thee I kneel,
    Maryland!
For life and death, for woe and weal,
Thy peerless chivalry reveal,
And gird thy beauteous limbs with steel,
    Maryland, my Maryland!
Thou wilt not cower in the dust,
    Maryland!
Thy beaming sword shall never rust,
    Maryland!
Remember Carroll's sacred trust,
Remember Howard's warlike thrust,
And all thy slumberers with the just,
    Maryland, my Maryland!
Come! 'tis the red dawn of the day,

Maryland!
Come with thy panoplied array,
Maryland!
With Ringgold's spirit for the fray,
With Watson's blood at Monterey,
With fearless Lowe and dashing May,
Maryland, my Maryland!
Dear Mother, burst the tyrant's chain,
Maryland!
Virginia should not call in vain,
Maryland!
She meets her sisters on the plain—
"*Sic semper!*" 'tis the proud refrain
That baffles minions back amain,
Maryland!
Arise in majesty again,
Maryland, my Maryland!
Come! for thy shield is bright and strong,
Maryland!
Come! for thy dalliance does thee wrong,
Maryland!
Come to thine own heroic throng
Stalking with Liberty along,
And chant thy dauntless slogan-song,
Maryland, my Maryland!
I see the blush upon thy cheek,
Maryland!
For thou wast ever bravely meek,
Maryland!

But lo! there surges forth a shriek,
From hill to hill, from creek to creek,
Potomac calls to Chesapeake,
    Maryland, my Maryland!
Thou wilt not yield the Vandal toll,
    Maryland!
Thou wilt not crook to his control,
    Maryland!
Better the fire upon thee roll,
Better the shot, the blade, the bowl,
Than crucifixion of the soul,
    Maryland, my Maryland!
I hear the distant thunder hum,
    Maryland!
The Old Line's bugle, fife and drum,
    Maryland!
She is not dead, nor deaf, nor dumb;
Huzza! she spurns the Northern scum!
She breathes! She burns! She'll come! She'll come!
    Maryland, my Maryland!

MAGDALEN

By JAMES RYDER RANDALL

The Hebrew girl, with flaming brow,
  The banner-blush of shame,

Sinks at the sinless Saviour's knees
And dares to breathe His name.
From the full fountain of her eyes
The lava-globes are roll'd—
They wash His feet; she spurns them off
With her ringlet-scarf of gold.

The Meek One feels the eloquence
Of agonizing prayer,
The burning tears, the suppliant face,
The penitential hair;
And when, to crown her brimming woe,
The ointment box is riven—
"Rise, daughter, rise! Much hast thou loved,
Be all thy sins forgiven!"

Dear God! The prayer of good and pure,
The canticles of light,
Enrobe Thy throne with gorgeous skies,
As incense in Thy sight;
May the shivered vase of Magdalen
Soothe many an outcast's smart,
Teaching what fragrant pleas may spring
From out a *broken heart!*

WHY THE ROBIN'S BREAST WAS RED

By James Ryder Randall

The Saviour, bowed beneath His Cross, climbed up the
    dreary hill,
And from the agonizing wreath ran many a crimson rill;
The cruel Roman thrust Him on with unrelenting hand,
Till, staggering slowly 'mid the crowd, He fell upon the sand.
A little bird that warbled near, that memorable day,
Flitted around and strove to wrench one single thorn away;
The cruel spike impaled his breast—and thus 'tis sweetly said,
The robin has his silver vest incarnadined with red.
Ah, Jesu! Jesu! Son of man! my dolor and my sighs
Reveal the lesson taught by this winged Ishmael of the skies.
I, in the palace of delight or cavern of despair,
Have plucked no thorns from Thy dear brow, but planted
    thousands there!

LE REPOS IN EGYPTE: THE SPHINX

By Agnes Repplier

All day I watch the stretch of burning sand;
    All night I brood beneath the golden stars;
Amid the silence of a desolate land,
    No touch of bitterness my reverie mars.

Built by the proudest of a kingly line,
  Over my head the centuries fly fast;
The secrets of the mighty dead are mine;
  I hold the key of a forgotten past.
Yet, ever hushed into a rapturous dream,
  I see again that night. A halo mild
Shone from the liquid moon. Beneath her beam
  Traveled a tired young Mother and the Child.
Within mine arms she slumbered, and alone
  I watched the Infant. At my feet her guide
Lay stretched o'er-wearied. On my breast of stone
  Rested the Crucified.

ANDROMEDA

By JAMES JEFFREY ROCHE

They chained her fair young body to the cold and cruel stone;
The beast begot of sea and slime had marked her for his own;
The callous world beheld the wrong, and left her there alone.
Base caitiffs who belied her, false kinsmen who denied her,
    Ye left her there alone!

My Beautiful, they left thee in thy peril and thy pain;
The night that hath no morrow was brooding on the main:
But, lo! a light is breaking of hope for thee again;
'Tis Perseus's sword a-flaming, thy dawn of day proclaiming

Across the western main.
O Ireland! O my country! he comes to break thy chain!

NATURE THE FALSE GODDESS

By JAMES JEFFREY ROCHE

The vilest work of vilest man,
    The cup that drugs, the sword that slays,
The purchased kiss of courtesan,
    The lying tongue of blame of praise,
The cobra's fang, the tiger's tongue,
    The python's murderous embrace—
The wrath of any living thing
    A man may fear but bravely face.
But thou, cold Mother, knowest naught
    Of love, of hate, or joy, or woe;
Thy bounties come to man unsought,
    Thy curses fall on friend and foe.
Thou bearest balm upon thy breath,
    Or sowest poison in the air;
And if man reapeth life or death,
    Thou dost not know, thou dost not care.
Thou art God's instrument of fate,
    Obedient, mighty, soulless, blind,
No demon to propitiate,
    No deity in love enshrined.

Let him who turns from God away
  To Bel or Moloch bend the knee;
Defile his soul to wood or clay,
  Or thrill with Voodoo's ecstasy.
Seek any fetich undivine,
  Be any superstition's thrall,
From Heaven or Hell will come a sign;
  But thou alone art deaf to all.

THREE DOVES

By JAMES JEFFREY ROCHE

Seaward, at morn, my doves flew free;
At eve they circled back to me.
The first was Faith; the second, Hope;
The third, the whitest, Charity.

Above the plunging surges play
Dream-like they hovered, day by day.
At last they turned, and bore to me
Green signs of peace thro' nightfall gray,

No shore forlorn, no loveliest land
Their gentle eye had left unscanned,
'Mid hues of twilight-heliotrope
Or daybreak fires by heaven-breath fanned

Quick visions of celestial grace—
Hither they waft, from earth's broad space,
Kind thoughts for all humanity,
They shine with radiance from God's face.

Ah, since my heart they choose for home,
Why loose them—forth again to roam?
Yet look; they rise with loftier scope
They wheel in flight toward Heaven's pure dome.

Fly, messengers that find no rest
Save in such toil as makes man blest!
Your home is God's immensity;
We hold you but at His behest.

THE WAY OF THE WORLD

By JAMES JEFFREY ROCHE

The hands of the King are soft and fair
   They never knew labor's strain
The hands of the Robber redly wear
   The bloody brand of Cain.
But the hands of the Man are hard and scarred
   With the scars of toil and pain.
The slaves of Pilate have washed his hands
   As white as a kings might be.

Barrabas with wrists unfettered stands
  For the world has made him free.
But Thy palms toil-worn by nails are torn,
  O Christ, on Calvary.

AVE MARIA

By JOHN JEROME ROONEY

Lady, thy soldier I would be,
  This day I choose thy shield,
And go, thrice-armored for the fight,
  Forth to the world's wide field.
There I shall meet the dark allies,
  The Flesh, the Fiend, the World,
And fiercely shall their darts of fire
  Upon my heart be hurled.

But I will raise my buckler strong
  Betwixt me and the foe,
And, with the spirit's flaming sword,
  Shall give them blow for blow.
Lady, thy sailor I would be,
  This day I sign my name
To sail the high seas of the earth
  For glory of thy fame.

The tempest may besiege my bark,
   The pirate lie in wait:
The perils of the monstrous deep
   May tempt o'erwhelming fate:
Yet, wheresoe'er my ship may steer
   Upon the waters wide,
Thy name shall be my compass sure,
   Thy star my midnight guide.

Thy poet, Lady, I would be
   To sing thy peerless praise;
Thy loyal bard, I'd bring to thee
   Heart-music from all lays.
Soft melody, outpoured in June
   By God's dear feathered throng,
Would mingle with the organ's roll
   To glorify my song;

And Dante's voice and Petrarch's strain
   And Milton's matchless line
Would lend to my poor minstrel note
   A harmony divine.
Lady, I choose to be thy son;
   For Mother thee I choose;
O, for thy sweet and holy Child,
   Do not my claim refuse!

Alone and motherless am I:
   Tho' strong, I long for rest—

The thunder of the world's applause
Is not a mother's breast.
Ave Maria! Shield us all.
Thy sons we choose to be.
Mother of grace, we raise our hearts,
Our hearts, our love to thee!

REVELATION

By JOHN JEROME ROONEY

*"And I saw a new heaven and a new earth: for the first heaven
and the first earth were passed away"* (REVELATION 21:1).

The Lord God said to His angel: "Let the old things pass
away.
They have heaped the earth with slaughter their sin obscures
the day.
Roll up the night on a curtain: let the stars fade one by one:
Out of the face of the heavens my anger shall blot the sun.
For the man I made and breathed on, filled with my breath
of breath,
Hath sown the seas with hatred, his skies are dark with death.
The babe is slain at the bosom, the babe who beholds
my face;
A welter of woe he leaves it—the dream of my love
and grace.

"Love was the dower I gave him, love the light of his days,
Love the core of his being, love, and the upward gaze.
Hate is the meat he feeds on, hate is his daily bread:
His drink is the blood of his brother, whom Cain hath
    stricken dead.
I said to the man in the Garden: 'Where is thy brother, Cain?'
'Am I my brother's keeper?' now comes the answer again."
The Lord God said to His angel: "This Thing is accursed
    and a lie:
It hath sinned from the Law I gave it, and surely it shall die."

"The Beasts of the field are patient, the birds rejoice in song—
But what is this Thing of blood-lust, and where does it
    belong?
Lo, I shall establish a judgment: Let the old things pass away:
They have heaped the fields with slaughter: their sin defiles
    the day.
They have laid on the weak sore burdens, on the just, their
    whips and ban:
For a handful of crimsoned silver they have kissed the Son
    of Man.
Roll back the scroll of the heavens; from out of the womb
    of birth
Come forth new heavens untainted; come forth, renewed,
    the Earth!"

MARQUETTE ON THE SHORES
OF THE MISSISSIPPI

(On seeing the original manuscript map of the
Mississippi River by its discoverer, Father Marquette.)

By JOHN JEROME ROONEY

Here, in the midnight of the solemn wood,
  He heard a roar as of a mighty wind—
  The onward rush of waters unconfined
Trampling in legions thro' the solitude.
Then lo! before him swept the conquering flood,
  Free as the freedom of the truth-strong mind
  Which hills of Doubt could neither hide nor bind,
Which, all in vain, the valley mounds withstood!

With glowing eye he saw the prancing tide
  With yellow mane rush onward thro' the night
  Into the vastness he had never trod:
Nor dreamt of conquest of that kingdom wide
  As down the flood his spirit took its flight
  Seeking the long-lost children of his God!

THE EMPIRE BUILDER

(*On the death of a Catholic gentleman.*)

By JOHN JEROME ROONEY

I.

This is the song of the Empire Builder,
Who out of the ends of the earth,
Thro' travail of war and of carnage
Brings strange, new realms to birth.
This is the boast of the Empire Builder:
Give heed to the deeds of his hands
And scorn thou not the glory he hath
In his gold and his wasted lands.
He hath counted his neighbors' cattle
With the cold, gray eye of greed:
He hath marked for his own the fields of wheat
Where he never had sown the seed:
The vine-clad cot by the hillside,
Where the farmer's children play—
"This shall fit in my plan," he said;
"What use for such as they?"
And so, in the dusk of evening,
He brought his arméd men,
And where had shone the clustering grapes
There stretched a waste again.
Homeless, the children wandered
Thro' the fields their father won:

No more shall they feel his clasp and kiss—
Aye, never beneath the sun.
Vex, vex not the Empire Builder,
Nor babble of Mercy's shield;
Hath he not his vaster issue—
The linking of field to field?
Hath he not noted the boundary
That lies 'twixt "mine and thine"?
Hath he not said, "'Twere better for thee
If thine henceforth be mine"?
And so doth the Empire Builder,
From out of the ends of the earth,
Thro' travail of war and of carnage
Bring strange, new realms to birth—
Realms builded on broken hearthstones,
The triumph of Rapine's hour—
That one may boast in the halls of Fame
And sit in the seats of Power!

II.

This is the song of the Empire Builder,
Who built not of wasted lands,
But who builded a kingdom of golden deeds
And of things not made by hands!
The fields of the spirit were his to roam,
The paths where the love-flowers grew:
He felt the breath of the spirits' spring
In every wind that blew:
It came not laden with dying groans

And homeless orphans' cries:
It blew from the mountains of the Lord
And the fields of Paradise.
This is the boast of the Empire Builder
Who built not of mouldering clay:
That the kingdom He built, not made by hands,
Shall never pass away!
The mind cannot measure its boundaries,
All Space is its outer gate:
It is broader than ever a man conceived
And more durable than Fate.
This is the Empire our brother built,
In His little hour of Earth,
Thro' the spirit's travail of righteous deeds
And the spirit's glad rebirth.
He had silenced the boast of the Empire Builder,
With his gold and wasted lands,
By his deathless kingdom of golden deeds
And of things not made by hands.
This is the kingdom our brother built:
It is good: it hath sufficed—
For who can measure the glory he keeps
With our Elder Brother, Christ?

THE MEN BEHIND THE GUNS

By JOHN JEROME ROONEY

A cheer and salute for the Admiral, and here's to the
   Captain bold,
And never forget the Commodore's debt when the deeds
   of might are told!
They stand to the deck through the battle's wreck when
   the great shells roar and screech—
And never they fear when the foe is near to practice what
   they preach:
But off with your hat and three times three for Columbia's
   true-blue sons,
The men below who batter the foe—the men behind
   the guns!

Oh, light and merry of heart are they when they swing into
   port once more,
When, with more than enough of the "green-backed stuff,"
   they start for their leave-o'-shore;
And you'd think, perhaps, that the blue-bloused chaps who
   loll along the street
Are a tender bit, with salt on it, for some fierce "mustache"
   to eat—
Some warrior bold, with straps of gold, who dazzles and
   fairly stuns
The modest worth of the sailor boys—the lads who serve
   the guns.

But say not a word till the shot is heard that tells the fight
   is on,
Till the long, deep roar grows more and more from the ships
   of "Yank" and "Don,"
Till over the deep the tempests sweep of fire and bursting
   shell,
And the very air is a mad despair in the throes of a living
   hell;
Then down, deep down, in the mighty ship, unseen by the
   midday suns,
You'll find the chaps who are giving the raps—the men
   behind the guns!

Oh, well they know the cyclones blow that they loose from
   their cloud of death,
And they know is heard the thunder-word their fierce
   ten-incher saith!
The steel decks rock with the lightning shock, and shake with
   the great recoil,
And the sea grows red with the blood of the dead and
   reaches for his spoil—
But not till the foe has gone below or turns his prow and runs
Shall the voice of peace bring sweet release to the men
   behind the guns!

A THOUGHT FROM CARDINAL NEWMAN†

By MATTHEW RUSSELL, S. J.

The world shines bright for inexperienced eyes,
   And death seems distant to the gay and strong,
   And in the youthful heart proud fancies throng,
And only present good can nature prize.
How then shall youth o'er these low vapours rise,
   And climb the upward path so steep and long?
   And how, amid earth's sights and sounds of wrong,
Walk with pure heart and face raised to the skies?

By gazing on the Infinitely Good,
   Whose love must quell, or hallow every other—
By living in the shadow of the Rood,
   For He that hangs there is our Elder Brother,
Who dying gave to us Himself as food,
   And His own Mother as our nursing Mother.

---

†   In the last of his "Discourses to Mixed Congregations," Dr. Newman calls the Blessed Virgin the Mother of Emanuel, and says: "It is the boast of the Catholic religion that it has the gift of making the young heart chaste; and why is this, but that it gives us Jesus for our food and Mary for our nursing Mother?"

THE CONQUERED BANNER

By ABRAM J. RYAN

Furl that Banner, for 'tis weary;
Round its staff 'tis drooping dreary:
    Furl it, fold it—it is best;
For there's not a man to wave it,
And there's not a sword to save it,
And there's not one left to lave it
In the blood which heroes gave it,
And its foes now scorn and brave it:
    Furl it, hide it—let it rest!
    Take that Banner down! 'tis tattered;
Broken is its staff and shattered;
And the valiant hosts are scattered,
    Over whom it floated high.
Oh, 'tis hard for us to fold it,
Hard to think there's none to hold it,
    Now must furl it with a sigh!
Furl that Banner!—furl it sadly!
Once ten thousands hailed it gladly,
And ten thousands wildly, madly,
    Swore it should forever wave;
Swore that foeman's sword should never
Hearts like theirs entwined dissever
Till that flag should float forever
    O'er their freedom or their grave!
Furl it! for the hands that grasped it,

And the hearts that fondly clasped it,
   Cold and dead are lying low;
And that Banner—it is trailing
While around it sounds the wailing
   Of its people in their woe.
For, though conquered, they adore it—
Love the cold, dead hands that bore it,
Weep for those who fell before it,
Pardon those who trailed and tore it;
And oh, wildly they deplore it.
   Now to furl and fold it so!
Furl that Banner! True, 'tis gory,
Yet 'tis wreathed around with glory,
And 'twill live in song and story
   Though its folds are in the dust!
For its fame on brightest pages,
Penned by poets and by sages,
Shall go sounding down the ages—
   Furl its folds though now we must.
Furl that Banner, softly, slowly!
Treat it gently—it is holy,
   For it droops above the dead.
Touch it not—unfold it never;
Let it droop there, furled forever—
   For its people's hopes are fled!

A CHILD'S WISH

By ABRAM J. RYAN

I wish I were the little key
   That locks Love's Captive in,
And lets Him out to go and free
   A sinful heart from sin.
I wish I were the little bell
   That tinkles for the Host,
When God comes down each day to dwell
   With hearts He loves the most.
I wish I were the chalice fair,
   That holds the Blood of Love,
When every gleam lights holy prayer
   Upon its way above.
I wish I were the little flower
   So near the Host's sweet face,
Or like the light that half an hour
   Burns on the shrine of grace.
I wish I were the altar where,
   As on His mother's breast,
Christ nestles, like a child, fore'er
   In Eucharistic rest.
But, oh, my God, I wish the most
   That my poor heart may be
A home all holy for each Host
   That comes in love to me.

THE SWORD OF ROBERT LEE

By ABRAM J. RYAN

Forth from its scabbard, pure and bright
  Flashed the sword of Lee!
Far in the front of the deadly fight,
High o'er the brave in the cause of Right,
Its stainless sheen, like a beacon bright,
  Led us to Victory.

Out of its scabbard, where, full long,
  It slumbered peacefully,
Roused from its rest by the battle's song,
Shielding the feeble, smiting the strong,
Guarding the right, avenging the wrong,
  Gleamed the sword of Lee.

Forth from its scabbard, high in air
  Beneath Virginia's sky—
And they who saw it gleaming there,
And knew who bore it, knelt to swear
That where that sword led they would dare
  To follow—and to die.

Out of its scabbard! Never hand
  Waved sword from stain as free,
Nor purer sword led braver band,
Nor braver bled for a brighter land,

Nor brighter land had a cause so grand,
  Nor cause a chief like Lee!

Forth from its scabbard! How we prayed
  That sword might victor be;
And when our triumph was delayed,
And many a heart grew sore afraid,
We still hoped on while gleamed the blade
  Of noble Robert Lee.

Forth from its scabbard all in vain
  Bright flashed the sword of Lee;
'Tis shrouded now in its sheath again,
It sleeps the sleep of our noble slain,
Defeated, yet without a stain,
  Proudly and peacefully.

SONG OF THE MYSTIC

By ABRAM J. RYAN

I walk down the Valley of Silence—
  Down the dim voiceless Valley—alone!
And I hear not the fall of a footstep
  Around me, save God's and my own;
And the hush of my heart is as holy
  As hovers where angels have flown!

Long ago was I weary of voices
  Whose magic my heart could not win;
Long ago was I weary of noises
  That fretted my soul with their din;
Long ago was I weary of places
  Where I met but the human—and sin.
I walked through the world with the worldly;
  I craved what the world never gave;
And I said: "In the world, each Ideal
  That shines like a star on life's wave,
Is wrecked on the shores of the Real,
  And sleeps like a dream in a grave."
And still did I pine for the Perfect,
  And still found the false with the true;
I sought 'mid the human for heaven,
  And caught a mere glimpse of its blue;
And I wept when the clouds of the mortal
  Veiled even that glimpse from my view.
And I toiled on, heart-tired of the Human;
  And I moaned 'mid the mazes of men;
Till I knelt, long ago, at an altar
  And heard a voice call me. Since then
I walk down the Valley of Silence
  That lies far beyond human ken.
Do you ask what I found in the Valley?
  'Tis my trysting-place with the Divine;
And I fell at the feet of the Holy,
  And above me a voice said: "Be mine!"
And there rose from the depths of my spirit

An echo—"My heart shall be thine."
Do you ask how I live in the Valley?
    I weep—and I dream—and I pray.
But my tears are as sweet as the dewdrops
    That fall on the roses in May;
And my prayers, like a perfume from censers,
    Ascendeth to God, night and day.
In the hush of the Valley of Silence,
    I dream all the songs that I sing;
And the music floats down the dim Valley,
    Till each finds a word for a wing,
That to men, like the Dove of the Deluge,
    A message of Peace they may bring.
But far on the deep there are billows
    That never shall break on the beach;
And I have heard songs in the Silence
    That never shall float into speech;
And I have had dreams in the Valley
    Too lofty for language to reach.
And I have seen Thoughts in the Valley—
    Ah, me! how my spirit was stirred!
And they wear holy veils on their faces,
    Their footsteps can scarcely be heard;
They pass through the Valley, like virgins
    Too pure for the touch of a word!
Do you ask me the place of the Valley,
    Ye hearts that are harrowed by Care?
It lieth afar, between mountains,
    And God and His angels are there;

And one is the dark mount of Sorrow,
And one the bright mountain of Prayer.

MARY, VIRGIN AND MOTHER

By E. Seton

Oh, Virgin Joy of all the world art thou,
In whose white, fragrant steps the countless throng
On souls elect doth follow God with song:
Creation's Queen, whose bright and holy brow
The multitude of Saints, like stars, endow
With changeful splendors, flashing far and strong:
The Maid unshadow'd by the primal wrong:
God's Lily, chosen in His shrine to bow.

All these thy glories are, and still a grace
More high, more dread, and yet more sweet and fair,
Doth bind thy royal brows, O Mary blest.
God called thee Mother; yea, His sacred face
The tender likeness of thine own doth wear.
And thou art ours—we trust Him for the rest.

THE WIND ON THE HILLS

By DORA SIGERSON

Go not to the hills of Erin
  When the night winds are about;
Put up your bar and shutter,
  And so keep the danger out.

For the good-folk whirl within it,
  And they pull by the hand,
And they push you by the shoulder,
  Till you move to their command.

And lo! you have forgotten
  What you have known of tears,
And you will not remember
  That the world goes full of years;

A year there is a lifetime,
  And a second but a day;
And an older world will greet you
  Each morn you come away.

Your wife grows old with weeping,
  And your children one by one
Grow grey with nights of watching,
  Before your dance is done.

And it will chance some morning
You will come home no more;
Your wife sees but a withered leaf
In the wind about the door.

And your children will inherit
The unrest of the wind;
They shall seek some face elusive,
And some land they never find.

When the wind is loud, they sighing
Go with hearts unsatisfied,
For some joy beyond remembrance,
For some memory denied.

And all your children's children,
They cannot sleep or rest,
When the wind is out in Erin
And the sun is in the West.

BELIEVE AND TAKE HEART

By JOHN LANCASTER SPALDING

What can console for a dead world?
We tread on dust which once was life;
To nothingness all things are hurled:

What meaning in a hopeless strife?
　　Time's awful storm
　　Breaks but the form.

Whatever comes, whatever goes,
Still throbs the heart whereby we live;
The primal joys still lighten woes,
And time which steals doth also give.
　　　　Fear not, be brave:
　　　　God can thee save.

The essential truth of life remains,
Its goodness and its beauty too,
Pure love's unutterable gains,
And hope which trills us through and through:
　　　　God has not fled,
　　　　Souls are not dead.

Not in most ancient Palestine,
Nor in the lightsome air of Greece,
Were human struggles more divine,
More blessed with guerdon of increase:
　　　　Take thou thy stand
　　　　In the workers' band.

Hast then no faith? Thine is the fault—
What prophets, heroes, sages, saints,
Have loved, on thee still makes assault,
Thee with immortal things acquaints.

On life then seize:
Doubt is disease.

AVE MARIA BELLS

By CHARLES WARREN STODDARD

At dawn, the joyful choir of bells,
In consecrated citadels,
Flings on the sweet and drowsy air
A brief, melodious call to prayer;
For Mary, Virgin meek and lowly,
Conceived of the Spirit Holy,
As the Lord's angel did declare.

At noon, above the fretful street,
Our souls are lifted to repeat
The prayer, with low and wistful voice:
"According to thy word and choice,
Though sorrowful and heavy laden,
So be it done to thy Handmaiden";
Then all the sacred bells rejoice.

At eve with roses in the west,
The daylight's withering bequest,
Ring, prayerful bells, while blossom bright

The stars, the lilies of the night:
  Of all the songs the years have sung us,
  "The Word made Flesh had dwelt among us,"
Is still our ever-new delight.

STIGMATA

By CHARLES WARREN STODDARD

In the wrath of the lips that assail us,
  In the scorn of the lips that are dumb,
The symbols of sorrow avail us,
  The joy of the people is come.
They parted Thy garments for barter,
  They follow Thy steps with complaint;
Let them know that the pyre of the martyr
  But purges the blood of the saint!

They have crucified Thee for a token,
  For a token Thy flesh crucified
Shall bleed in a heart that is broken
  For love of the wound in Thy side;
In pity for palms that were pleading,
  For feet that were grievously used,
There is blood on the brow that is bleeding
  And torn, as Thy brow that was bruised!
By Thee have we life, breath, and being;

Thou hast knowledge of us and our kind;
Thou hast pleasure of eyes that are seeing,
And sorrow of eyes that are blind;
By the seal of the mystery shown us—
　The wound that with Thy wounds accord—
O Lord, have mercy upon us!
　Have mercy upon us, O Lord!

THE BELLS OF SAN GABRIEL

By CHARLES WARREN STODDARD

(*The Mission of San Gabriel Archangel, near Los Angeles, founded in 1771, was, for a time, the most flourishing mission in California.*)

Thine was the corn and the wine,
　The blood of the grape that nourished;
The blossom and fruit of the vine
　That was heralded far away.
　When the wine and fig-tree flourished,
The promise of peace and of glad increase
　Forever and ever and aye.
What then wert thou, and what art now?
　Answer me, O, I pray!

　　And every note of every bell
　　Sang Gabriel! rang Gabriel!

In the tower that is left the tale to tell
  Of Gabriel, the Archangel.

Oil of the olive was thine;
  Flood of the wine-press flowing,
Blood of the Christ was the wine—
  Blood of the Lamb that was slain.
Thy gifts were fat of the kine
  Forever coming and going
Far over the hills, the thousand hills—
  Their lowing a soft refrain.
What then wert thou, and what art now?
  Answer me once again!

  And every note of every bell
    Sang Gabriel! rang Gabriel!
  In the tower that is left the tale to tell
    Of Gabriel, the Archangel.

Seed of the corn was thine—
  Body of Him thus broken
And mingled with blood of the vine—
  The bread and the wine of life.
Out of the good sunshine
  They were given to thee as a token—
The body of Him, and the blood of Him,
  When the gifts of God were rife.
What then wert thou, and what art now?
  After the weary strife?

And every note of every bell
Sang Gabriel! rang Gabriel!
In the tower that is left the tale to tell
Of Gabriel, the Archangel.

Where are they now, O bells?
Where are the fruits of the Mission?
Garnered, where no one dwells,
Shepherd and flock are fled.
O'er the Lord's vineyard swells
The tide that with fell perdition
Sounded their doom and fashioned their tomb
And buried them with the dead.
What then wert thou, and what art now?
The answer is still unsaid.

And every note of every bell
Sang Gabriel! rang Gabriel!
In the tower that is left the tale to tell
Of Gabriel, the Archangel.

Where are they now, O tower!
The locusts and wild honey?
Where is the sacred dower
That the bride of Christ was given?
Gone to the wielders of power,
The misers and minters of money;
Gone for the greed that is their creed—
And these in the land have thriven.

What then wert thou, and what art now,
And wherefore hast thou striven?

And every note of every bell
Sang Gabriel! rang Gabriel!
In the tower that is left the tale to tell
Of Gabriel, the Archangel.

THE POOR

By SPEER STRAHAN, C.S.C.

The poor I saw at the cloister gate
Mutely beg with their patient eyes
An alms, for the love of Him who sate
And supped with the poor in human guise.

And there were monks saw the nails' deep scars
In the shrunken hands that reached for bread,
Who heard a Voice from beyond the stars
In the broken thanks of them they fed.

I, too, at the gates of God each day
Seek for an alms of strength and grace,
Beggar am I that wait and pray
To feast my soul on His beauteous Face.

THE PROMISED COUNTRY

By SPEER STRAHAN, C.S.C.

Fair must that promised country be
Whose streams rise from eternity
And One doth lead upon that way
Whose footfalls are the paths of day.

Nor lurking fear pursues them there,
As forward in the morning air
With Him the blessed ransomed go,
Their garments washen white as snow.

Alas! my days are very dim
That look up to the Seraphim.
Ah, Lord, some dawning may I be
One of that shining company!

HOLY COMMUNION

By SPEER STRAHAN, C.S.C.

Disguised He stands without in the street;
Far come is He on heavy feet.
O heart of mine, open thy gate;
For darkness falls, and it is late!

Lord of the heaven's fairest height,
Homeless in the traveler's night,
Begging my hearth, my board, my cup,
That I, not He, may richly sup.

O soul of mine, the board begin,
And let this wondrous Beggar in!

STARS OF CHEER

By CAROLINE D. SWAN

The silent Christmas stars shine cool and clear
　Above a world of mingled joy and woe;
　On peaceful cottage homes, with thanks aglow
For royal bounty of the grape-crowned year;
And on red fields of blood, where many a tear
　Is wiped away by Death, a gentle foe,
　More merciful than they who bade it flow.
Shine, silver stars, rain down your blessed cheer!

Comfort the mourner with your Angel song!
The Christ-Child reigns. Behold His tiny hand
　Upraised in benediction warm and sweet!
O'er every joy and every bitter wrong
　The Babe of Bethlehem hath supreme command;
　　Come, worship, kings and peoples, at His feet!

CHRIST AND THE PAGAN

By JOHN B. TABB

I had no God but these,
The sacerdotal Trees,
And they uplifted me.
"*I hung upon a tree.*"

The sun and moon I saw,
And reverential awe
Subdued me day and night.
"*I am the perfect light.*"

Within a lifeless Stone—
All other gods unknown—
I sought Divinity.
"*The Corner-Stone am I.*"

For sacrificial feast
I slaughtered man and beast,
Red recompense to gain.
"*So I, a Lamb, was slain.*

Yea; such My hungering Grace
That where ev'r My face
Is hidden, none may grope
Beyond eternal Hope."

OUT OF BOUNDS

By JOHN B. TABB

A little Boy of heavenly birth,
  But far from home today,
Comes down to find His ball, the Earth,
  That Sin has cast away.
O comrades, let us one and all
Join in to get Him back His ball!

FATHER DAMIEN

By JOHN B. TABB

O God, the cleanest offering
Of tainted earth below,
Unblushing to Thy feet we bring—
"A leper white as snow!"

RECOGNITION

By JOHN B. TABB

When Christ went up to Calvary,
  His crown upon His head,
Each tree unto its fellow-tree

In awful silence said:
"Behold the Gardener is He
Of Eden and Gethsemane!"

"IS THY SERVANT A DOG?"

By JOHN B. TABB

So *must* he be, who in the crowded street,
Where shameless Sin and flaunting Pleasure meet,
Amid the noisome footprints finds the sweet
Faint vestige of Thy feet.

LILIUM REGIS

By FRANCIS THOMPSON

O Lily of the King, low lies thy silver wing,
And long has been the hour of thine unqueening;
And thy scent of Paradise on the night-wind spends its sighs,
Nor any take the secrets of its meaning.
O Lily of the King, I speak a heavy thing,
O patience, most sorrowful of daughters!
Lo, the hour is at hand for the troubling of the land,
And red shall be the breaking of the waters.
Sit fast upon thy stalk, when the blast shall with thee talk,
With the mercies of the King for thine awning,

And the Just understand that thine hour is at hand,
Thine hour at hand with power in the dawning.
When the nations lie in blood, and their kings a broken brood,
Look up, O most sorrowful of daughters!
Lift up thy head and hark what sounds are in the dark,
For His feet are coming to thee on the waters.
O Lily of the King, I shall not see that sing,
I shall not see the hour of thy queening!
But my Song shall see, and wake like a flower that
    dawn-winds shake,
And sigh with joy the odours of its meaning.
O Lily of the King, remember then the thing
That this dead mouth sang; and thy daughters,
As they dance before His way; sing there on the Day
What I sang when night was on the waters!

TO THE ENGLISH MARTYRS

By FRANCIS THOMPSON

Rain, rain on Tyburn tree,
Red rain a-falling;
Dew, dew on Tyburn tree,
Red dew on Tyburn tree,
And the swart bird a-calling.
The shadow lies on England now
Of the deathly-fruited bough:

Cold and black with malison
Lies between the land and sun;
Putting out the sun, the bough
Shades England now!
The troubled heavens so wan with care,
And burdened with the earth's despair
Shiver a-cold; the starved heaven
Has want, with wanting men bereaven.
Blest fruit of the unblest bough,
Aid the land that smote you, now!
That feels the sentence and the curse
Ye died if so ye might reverse.
When God was stolen from out man's mouth,
Stolen was the bread; then hunger and drouth
Went to and fro; began the wail,
Struck root the poor-house and the jail,
Ere cut the dykes, let through that flood,
Ye writ the protest with your blood;
Against this night—wherein our breath
Withers, and the toiled heart perisheth—
Entered the *caveat* of your death.
Christ in the form of His true Bride,
Again hung pierced and crucified,
And groaned, "I thirst!" Not still ye stood—
Ye had your hearts, ye had your blood;
And pouring out the eager cup—
"The wine is weak, yet, Lord Christ, sup."
Ah, blest! who bathed the parched Vine
With richer than His Cana-wine,

And heard, your most sharp supper past:
"Ye kept the best wine to the last!"
Ah, happy who
That sequestered secret knew,
How sweeter than bee-haunted dells
The blosmy blood of martyrs smells!
Who did upon the scaffold's bed,
The ceremonial steel between you, wed
With God's grave proxy, high and reverend Death;
Or felt about your neck, sweetly,
(While the dull horde
Saw but the unrelenting cord)
The Bridegroom's arm, and that long kiss
That kissed away your breath, and claimed you His.
You did, with thrift of holy gain,
Unvenoming the sting of pain,
Hive its sharp heather-honey. Ye
Had sentience of the mystery
To make Abaddon's hooked wings
Buoy you up to starry things;
Pain of heart, and pain of sense,
Pain the scourge, ye taught to cleanse;
Pain the loss became possessing;
Pain the curse was pain the blessing.
Chains, rack, hunger, solitude—these,
Which did your soul from earth release,
Left it free to rush upon
And merge in its compulsive Sun.
Desolated, bruised, forsaken,

Nothing taking, all things taken,
Lacerated and tormented,
The stifled soul, in naught contented,
On all hands straitened, cribbed, denied,
Can but fetch breath o' the Godward side.
Oh, to me, give but to me
That flower of felicity,
Which on your topmost spirit ware
The difficult and snowy air
Of high refusal! and the heat
Of central love which fed with sweet
And holy fire i' the frozen sod
Roots that ta'en hold on God.
Unwithering youth in you renewed
Those rosy waters of your blood—
The true *Fons Juventutis*; ye
Pass with conquest that Red Sea,
And stretch out your victorious hand
Over the Fair and Holy Land.
O by the Church's pondering art
Late set and named upon the chart
Of her divine astronomy,
Through your influence from on high
Long shed unnoted! Bright
New cluster in our Northern night,
Cleanse from its pain and undelight
An impotent and tarnished hymn,
Whose marish exhalations dim
Splendours they would transfuse! And thou

Kindle the words which blot thee now,
Over whose sacred corse unhearsed
Europe veiled her face, and cursed
The regal mantle grained in gore
Of genius, freedom, faith, and More!
Ah, happy Fool of Christ, unawed
By familiar sanctities,
You served your Lord at holy ease!
Dear Jester in the Courts of God—
In whose spirit, enchanting yet,
Wisdom and love together met,
Laughed on each other for content!
That an inward merriment,
An inviolate soul of pleasure,
To your motions taught a measure
All your days; which tyrant king,
Nor bonds, nor any bitter thing,
Could embitter or perturb;
No daughter's tears, nor, more acerb,
A daughter's frail declension from
Thy serene example, come
Between thee and thy much content.
Nor could the last sharp argument
Turn thee from thy sweetest folly;
To the keen *accolade* and holy
Thou didst bend low a sprightly knee,
And jest Death out of gravity
As a too sad-visaged friend;
So, jocund passing to the end

Of thy laughing martyrdom;
And now from travel art gone home
Where, since gain of thee was given,
Surely there is more mirth in heaven!
Thus, in Fisher and in thee,
Arose the purple dynasty,
The anointed Kings of Tyburn tree;
High in act and word each one:
He that spake—and to the sun
Pointed—"I shall shortly be
Above yon fellow," He too, he
No less high of speech and brave,
Whose word was: "Though I shall have
Sharp dinner, yet I trust in Christ
To have a most sweet supper." Priced
Much by men that utterance was
Of the doomed Leonidas—
Not more exalt than these, which note
Men who thought as Shakespeare wrote.
But more lofty eloquence
Than is writ by poet's pens
Lives in your great deaths: O these
Have more fire than poesies!
And more ardent than all ode,
The pomps and raptures of your blood!
By that blood ye hold in fee
This earth of England; Kings are ye:
And ye have armies—Want, and Cold,
And heavy Judgments manifold

Hung in the unhappy air, and Sins
That the sick gorge to heave begins,
Agonies and Martyrdoms,
Love, Hope, Desire, and all that comes
From the unwatered soul of man
Gaping on God. These are the van
Of conquest, these obey you; these,
And all the strengths of weaknesses,
That brazen walls disbed. Your hand,
Princes, put forth to the command,
And levy upon the guilty land
Your saving wars; on it go down,
Black beneath God's and heaven's frown;
Your prevalent approaches make
With unsustainable grace, and take
Captive the land that captived you;
To Christ enslave ye and subdue
Her so bragged freedom: for the crime
She wrought on you in antique time,
Parcel the land among you; reign,
Viceroys to your sweet Suzerain!
Till she shall know
This lesson in her overthrow:
Hardest servitude has he
That's jailed in arrogant liberty;
And freedom, spacious and unflawed,
Who is walled about with God.

THE HOUND OF HEAVEN

By FRANCIS THOMPSON

I fled Him, down the nights and down the days;
  I fled Him down the arches of the years;
  I fled Him down the labrinthine ways
    Of my own mind; and in the midst of tears
I hid from Him, and under running laughter.
      Up vistaed hopes I sped;
      And shot, precipitated,
    Adown Titanic glooms of chasmed fears,
From those strong Feet that followed, followed after.
      But with unhurrying chase,
      And unperturbed pace,
    Deliberate speed, majestic instancy,
      They beat—and a Voice beat
      More instant than the Feet—
"All things betray thee, who betrayest Me."

      I pleaded, outlaw-wise,
By many a hearted casement, curtained red,
  Trellised with intertwining charities;
(For, though I knew His love Who followed,
      Yet was I sore adread
Lest, having Him, I must have naught beside);
But, if one little casement parted wide.
  The gust of His approach would clash it to.
Fear wist not to evade, as Love wist to pursue.

Across the margent of the world I fled,
   And troubled the gold gateway of the stars,
   Smiting for shelter on their clanged bars;
      Fretted to dulcet jars
And silvern chatter the pale ports o' the moon.
I said to dawn, Be sudden; to eve, Be soon;
   With thy young skiey blossoms heap me over
      From this tremendous Lover!
Float thy vague veil about me, lest He see!
   I tempted all His servitors, but to find
My own betrayal in their constancy,
In faith to Him their fickleness to me,
   Their traitorous trueness, and their loyal deceit.
To all swift things for swiftness did I sue;
   Clung to the whistling mane of every wind.
      But whether they swept, smoothly fleet,
   The long savannahs of the blue;
      Or whether, Thunder-driven,
   They clanged his chariot 'thwart a heaven
Plashy with flying lightnings round the spurn o' their feet—
   Fear wist not to evade as Love wist to pursue.
      Still with unhurrying chase,
      And unperturbed pace,
   Deliberate speed, majestic instancy,
      Came on the following Feet,
      And a Voice above their beat—
   "Naught shelters thee, who wilt not shelter Me."

I sought no more that after which I strayed
  In face of man or maid;
But still within the little children's eyes
  Seems something, something that replies;
They at least are for me, surely for me!
I turned me to them very wistfully;
But, just as their young eyes grew sudden fair
  With dawning answers there,
Their angel plucked them from me by the hair.
"Come then, ye other children, Nature's—share
With me" (said I) "your delicate fellowship;
    Let me greet you lip to lip,
    Let me twine with you caresses,
    Wantoning
    With our Lady-Mother's vagrant tresses,
    Banqueting
    With her in her wind-walled palace,
    Underneath her azured dais,
    Quaffing, as your taintless way is,
    From a chalice
Lucent-weeping out of the day spring."
    So it was done:
I in their delicate fellowship was one—
Drew the bolt of Nature's secrecies.
I knew all the swift importings
    On the wilful face of skies;
    I knew how the clouds arise
    Spumed of the wild sea-snortings;

All that's born or dies
    Rose and drooped with—made them shapers
Of mine own moods, or wailful or divine—
    With them joyed and was bereaven.
    I was heavy with the even,
    When she lit her glimmering tapers
    Round the day's dead sanctities.
    I laughed in the morning's eyes.
I triumphed and I saddened with all weather,
    Heaven and I wept together,
And its sweet tears were salt with mortal mine;
Against the red throb of its sunset-heart
    I laid my own to beat,
    And share commingling heat;
But not by that, by that, was eased my human smart.
In vain my tears were wet on Heaven's grey cheek.
For ah, we know not what each other says
    These things and I; in sound *I* speak—
Their sound is but their stir, they speak by silences.
Nature, poor stepdame, cannot slake my drought;
    Let her, if she would owe me,
Drop yon blue bosom-veil of sky, and show me
    The breasts of her tenderness:
Never did any milk of hers once bless
    My thirsting mouth.
    Nigh and nigh draws the chase,
    With unperturbed pace,
    Deliberate speed, majestic instancy;
    And past those noised fleet—

A Voice comes yet more fleet—
"Lo! naught contents thee who content'st not Me."

Naked I wait Thy love's uplifted stroke!
My harness piece by piece Thou hast hewn from me,
     I am defenceless utterly.
     I slept, methinks, and woke,
And, slowly gazing, find me stripped in sleep.
In the rash lustihead of my young powers,
     I shook the pillaring hours
And pulled my life upon me; grimed with smears,
I stand amid the dust o' the mounded years—
My mangled youth lies dead beneath the heap.
My days have crackled and gone up in smoke,
Have puffed and burst as sun-starts on a stream.
     Yea, faileth now even dream
The dreamer, and the lute the lutanist;
Even the linked fantasies, in whose blossomy twist
I swung the earth a trinket at my wrist,
Are yielding; cords of all too weak account
For earth with heavy griefs so overplussed.
     Ah! is Thy love indeed
A weed, albeit an amaranthine weed,
Suffering no flowers except its own to mount?
     Ah! must—
     Designer infinite!
Ah! must Thou char the wood ere Thou canst limn with it?
My freshness spent its wavering shower i' the dust;
And now my heart is as a broken fount,

Wherein tear-drippings stagnate, spilt down ever
  From the dank thoughts that shiver
Upon the sighful branches of my mind.
  Such is; what is to be?
The pulp so bitter, how shall taste the rind?
I dimly guess what Time in mists confounds;
Yet ever and anon a trumpet sounds
From the hid battlements of Eternity;
Those shaken mists a space unsettle, then
Round the half-glimpsed turrets slowly wash again.
  But not ere him who summoneth
  I first have seen enwound
With glooming robes purpureal, cypress-crowned;
His name I know, and what his trumpet saith.
Whether man's heart or life it be which yields
  Thee harvest, must Thy harvest fields
  Be dunged with rotten death?
  Now of that long pursuit
  Comes on at hand the bruit;
That Voice is round me like a bursting sea:
  "And is thy earth so marred,
  Shattered in shard on shard?
 Lo! all things fly thee, for thou fliest Me!
 Strange, piteous, futile thing,
Wherefore should any set thee love apart?
Seeing none but I makes much of naught" (He said)
"And human love needs human meriting:
  How hast thou merited—
Of all man's clotted clay the dingiest clot?

Alack, thou knowest not
How little worthy of any love thou art!
Whom wilt thou find to love ignoble thee
    Save Me, save only Me?
All which I took from thee I did but take,
    Not for thy harms,
But just that thou might'st seek it in My arms.
    All which thy child's mistake
Fancies as lost, I have stored for thee at home:
    Rise, clasp My hand, and come!"

    Halts by me that footfall:
    Is my gloom, after all,
Shade of His hand, outstretched caressingly?
    "Ah, fondest, blindest, weakest,
    I am He Whom thou seekest!
Thou dravest love from thee, who dravest Me."

THE DREAD OF HEIGHT

By FRANCIS THOMPSON

*"If ye were blind, ye should have no sin: but now ye say;
We see: your sin remaineth"* (JOHN 9:41).

Not the Circean wine
Most perilous is for pain:

Grapes of the heaven's star-loaden vine,
Whereto the lofty-placed
Thoughts of fair souls attain,
Tempt with a more retributive delight,
And do disrelish all life's sober taste.

'Tis to have drunk too well
The drink that is divine,
Maketh the kind earth waste,
And breath intolerable.

Ah, me!
How shall my mouth content it with mortality?
Lo, secret music, sweetest music,
From distances of distance drifting its lone flight,
Down the arcane where Night would perish in night,
Like a god's loosened locks slips undulously:
Music that is too grievous of the height
For safe and low delight,
Too infinite
For bounded hearts which yet would girth the sea!
So let it be,
Though sweet be great, and though my heart be small:
So let it be,
O music, music, though you wake in me
No joy, no joy at all;
Although you only wake
Uttermost sadness, measure of delight,
Which else I could not credit to the height,

Did I not know,
Did I not know,
That ill is statured to its opposite;
And even of sadness so,
Of utter sadness, make
Of extreme sad a rod to mete
The incredible excess of unsensed sweet,
And mystic wall of strange felicity.
So let it be,
Though sweet be great, and though my heart be small,
And bitter meat
The food of Gods for men to eat;
Yea, John ate daintier, and did tread
Less ways of heat,
Than whom to their wind-carpeted
High banquet hall,
And golden love-feasts, the fair stars entreat.

But ah! withal,
Some hold, some stay,
O difficult joy, I pray,
Some arms of thine,
Not only, only arms of mine!
Lest like a weary girl I fall
From clasping love so high,
And lacking thus thine arms, then may
Most hapless I
Turn utterly to love of basest rate;
For low they fall whose fall is from the sky.

Yea, who me shall secure
But I, of height grown desperate,
Surcease my wing, and my lost fate
Be dashed from pure
To broken writhings in the shameful slime:
Lower than man, for I dreamed higher,
Thrust down, by how much I aspire,
And damned with drink of immortality?
For such things be,
Yea, and the lowest reach of reeky Hell
Is but made possible
By foreta'en breath of Heaven's austerest clime.

These tidings from the vast to bring
Needeth not doctor nor divine,
Too well, too well
My flesh doth know the heart-perturbing thing;
That dread theology alone
Is mine,
Most native and my own;
And ever with victorious toil
When I have made
Of the delfic peaks dim escalade,
My soul with anguish and recoil
Doth like a city in an earthquake rock,
As at my feet the abyss is cloven then,
With deeper menace than for other men,
Of my potential cousinship with mire;
That all my conquered skies do grow a hollow mock,

My fearful powers retire,
No longer strong,
Reversing the shook banners of their song.

Ah, for a heart less native to high Heaven,
A hooded eye, for jesses and restraint,
Or for a will accipitrine to pursue!—
The veil of tutelar flesh to simple livers given,
Or those brave-fledging fervours of the Saint,
Whose heavenly falcon-craft doth never taint,
Nor they in sickest time their ample virtue mew.

TO MY GODCHILD—FRANCIS M. W. M.

By FRANCIS THOMPSON

This labouring, vast, Tellurian galleon,
Riding at anchor off the orient sun,
Had broken its cable, and stood out to space
Down some froze Arctic of the aerial ways:
And now, back warping from the inclement main,
Its vapourous shroudage drenched with icy rain,
It swung into its azure roads again;
When, floated on the prosperous sun-gale, you
Lit, a white halcyon auspice, 'mid our frozen crew.

To the Sun, stranger, surely you belong,
Giver of golden days and golden song;

Nor is it by an all-unhappy plan
You bear the name of me, his constant Magian.
Yet, ah! from any other that it came,
Lest fated to my fate you be, as to my name.
When at the first those tidings did they bring,
My heart turned troubled at the ominous thing:
Though well may such a title him endower,
For when a poet's prayer implores a poet's power.
The Assisian, who kept plighted faith to three,
To Song, to Sanctitude, and Poverty,
(In two alone of whom most singers prove
A fatal faithfulness of during love!);
He the sweet Sales, of whom we scarcely ken
How God he could love more, he so loved men;
The crown and crowned of Laura and Italy;
And Fletcher's fellow—from these, and not from me,
Take you your name, and take your legacy!

Or, if a right successive you declare
When worms, for ivies, intertwine my hair,
Take but this Poesy that now followeth
My clayey best with sullen servile breath,
Made then your happy freedman by testating death.
My song I do but hold for you in trust,
I ask you but to blossom from my dust.
When you have compassed all weak I began,
Diviner poet, and ah! diviner man—
The man at feud with the perduring child
In you before song's altar nobly reconciled—

From the wise heavens I half shall smile to see
How little a world, which owned you, needed me.
If, while you keep the vigils of the night,
For your wild tears make darkness all too bright,
Some lone orb through your lonely window peeps,
As it played lover over your sweet sleeps,
Think it a golden crevice in the sky,
Which I have pierced but to behold you by!

And when, immortal mortal, droops your head,
And you, the child of deathless song, are dead;
Then, as you search with unaccustomed glance
The ranks of Paradise for my countenance,
Turn not your tread along the Uranian sod
Among the bearded counsellors of God;
For, if in Eden as on earth are we,
I sure shall keep a younger company:
Pass where beneath their ranged gonfalons
The starry cohorts shake their shielded suns,
The dreadful mass of their enridged spears:
Pass where majestical the eternal peers,
The stately choice of the great Saintdom, meet—
A silvern segregation, globed complete
In sandalled shadow of the Triune feet;
Pass by where wait, young poet-wayfarer,
Your cousined clusters, emulous to share
With you the roseal lightnings burning 'mid their hair;
Pass the crystalline sea, the Lampads seven—
Look for me in the nurseries of Heaven.

MICHAEL THE ARCHANGEL

By KATHERINE TYNAN

Not woman-faced and sweet, as look
The angels in the picture-book;
But terrible in majesty,
More than an army passing by.

His hair floats not upon the wind
Like theirs, but curled and closely twined;
Wrought with his aureole, so that none
Shall know the gold curls from the crown.

His wings he hath put away in steel,
He goes mail-clad from head to heel;
Never moon-silver hath outshone
His breastplate and his morion.

His brows are like a battlement,
Beautiful, brave and innocent;
His eyes with fires of battle burn—
On his strong mouth the smile is stern.

His horse, the horse of Heaven, goes forth,
Bearing him off to South and North,
Neighing far off, as one that sees
The battle over distances.

His fiery sword is never at rest,
His foot is in the stirrup prest;
Through all the world where wrong is done
Michael the Soldier rideth on.

Michael, Commander! Angels are
That sound the trumpet and that bear
The banners by the Throne, where is
The King one nameth on his knees.

Angels there are of peace and prayers,
And they that go with wayfarers,
And they that watch the house of birth,
And they that bring the dead from earth.

And mine own Angel. Yet I see,
Heading God's army gloriously,
Michael Archangel, like a sun,
Splendid beyond comparison!

PLANTING BULBS

By KATHERINE TYNAN

Setting my bulbs a-row
    In cold earth under the grasses,
Till the frost and the snow
    Are gone and the Winter passes—

Sudden a footfall light,
  Sudden a bird-call ringing;
And these in gold and in white
  Shall rise with a sound of winging.

Airy and delicate all,
  All go trooping and dancing
At Spring's call and footfall,
  Airily dancing, advancing.

In the dark of the year,
  Turning the earth so chilly,
I look to the day of cheer,
  Primrose and daffodilly.

Turning the sods and the clay
  I think on the poor sad people
Hiding their dead away
  In the churchyard, under the steeple.

All poor women and men,
  Broken-hearted and weeping,
Their dead they call on in vain,
  Quietly smiling and sleeping.

Friends, now listen and hear,
  Give over crying and grieving,
There shall come a day and a year
  When the dead shall be as the living.

There shall come a call, a footfall,
   And the golden trumpeters blowing
Shall stir the dead with their call,
   Bid them be rising and going.

Then in the daffodil weather
   Lover shall run to lover;
Friends all trooping together;
   Death and Winter be over.

Laying my bulbs in the dark,
   Visions have I of hereafter.
Lip to lip, breast to breast, hark!
   No more weeping, but laughter!

SHEEP AND LAMBS

By KATHERINE TYNAN

All in the April evening,
   April airs were abroad;
The sheep with their little lambs
   Passed me by on the road.
The sheep with their little lambs
   Passed me by on the road;
All in the April evening
   I thought on the Lamb of God.

The lambs were weary, and crying
　With a weak, human cry.
I thought on the Lamb of God
　Going meekly to die.
Up in the blue, blue mountains
　Dewy pastures are sweet;
Rest for the little bodies,
　Rest for the little feet.

But for the Lamb of God
　Up on a hilltop green
Only a cross of shame
　Two stark crosses between.
All in the April evening,
　April airs were abroad;
I saw the sheep with their lambs,
　And thought on the Lamb of God.

THE MAKING OF BIRDS

By KATHERINE TYNAN

God made Him birds in a pleasant humour;
　Tired of planets and suns was He.
He said: "I will add a glory to summer,
　Gifts for my creatures banished from Me!"

He had a thought and it set Him smiling
  Of the shape of a bird and its glancing head,
Its dainty air and its grace beguiling:
  "I will make feathers," the Lord God said.

He made the robin; He made the swallow;
  His deft hands moulding the shape to His mood,
The thrush and the lark and the finch to follow,
  And laughed to see that His work was good.

He Who has given men gift of laughter,
  Made in His image; He fashioned fit
The blink of the owl and the stork thereafter,
  The little wren and the long-tailed tit.

He spent in the making His wit and fancies;
  The wing-feathers He fashioned them strong;
Deft and dear as daisies and pansies,
  He crowned His work with the gift of song.

"Dearlings," He said, "make songs for my praises!"
  He tossed them loose to the sun and the wind,
Airily sweet as pansies and daisies;
  He taught them to build a nest to their mind.

The dear Lord God of His glories weary—
  Christ our Lord had the heart of a boy—
Made Him birds in a moment merry,
  Bade them soar and sing for His joy.

THE MAN OF THE HOUSE

By KATHERINE TYNAN

Joseph, honoured from sea to sea,
This is your name that pleases me,
    "Man of the House."

I see you rise at the dawn and light
The fire and blow till the flame is bright.
I see you take the pitcher and carry
The deep well-water for Jesus and Mary.

You knead the corn for the bread so fine,
Gather them grapes from the hanging vine.
There are little feet that are soft and slow,
Follow you whithersoever you go.

There's a little face at your workshop door,
A little one sits down on your floor:
Holds His hands for the shavings curled,
The soft little hands that have made the world.

Mary calls you: the meal is ready:
You swing the Child to your shoulder steady.
I see your quiet smile as you sit
And watch the little Son thrive and eat.

The vine curls by the window space,
The wings of angels cover the face.
Up in the rafters, polished and olden,
There's a Dove that broods and his wings are golden.

You who kept Them through shine and storm,
A staff, a shelter kindly and warm,
Father of Jesus, husband of Mary,
Hold us your lilies for sanctuary!

Joseph, honoured from sea to sea,
Guard me mine and my own roof-tree,
    "Man of the House"!

CAELO ET IN TERRA

By THOMAS WALSH

Earth is a jealous mother; from her breast
She will endure no separation long
From aught she bore;
So one by one
She claimeth evermore
The parent and the friend—
The loveliest and the best,
The meek, the faithful, and the strong—
Till, link by golden link undone,

The very tomb that seems
To youth the dismal gulf of all that's fair,
Becomes the chosen hearthstone of our dreams,
The wonder-house of all most rare,
Most deathless, and most dear;
Where the bereaved heart,
Life's exile held apart,
Would turn for love-warmth and abiding cheer.
Yea—earth can be so kind—
Then ye that rule the wind,
Are ye of less appeal?
Ye spirits of the stars
And regions where the suns
Themselves as atoms wheel
Beneath your thundering cars?
Cerulean ones!—
Or goddesses, or saints,
Or demiurge, or Trinities,
Wherewith heaven highest faints!
Are ye less kind than these
Dim vaults of clay,
Ye boasts and fathers of the ancient day?
Thou god Avernian, Dis!—behold
What timid form and old
Adown thy purple gulf descends
Unto the arch of Death—(Grim friend of friends!
Be thou placated!) 'Tis a mother, see,
Takes her first step—a child—into eternity!
Leave her not fearful there

Who was of love entire,
So gentle and so fair!—
Thy majesty and dread withhold
For the high head and bold—
Imperial Death, mock not thyself with ire!
Nay—then it was not fear
That stayed her foot the while;
For now her lovely eyes,
Unclouded, brown,
Are lighted with their greeting smile—
The Hand awaited through the gloom
Is seen!—her whitened forehead lies
Upon the Shepherd's shoulder down—
Yea—her own Jesus comes—to lead
Unto the meadows where is Peace indeed!

EGIDIO OF COIMBRA—1597 A.D.

By THOMAS WALSH

The rumor came to Frei Egidio
In cloistered Santa Cruz, that out of Spain
King Philips secret courier had fared
With orders under seal suspending all
The statutes of Coimbra that controlled
The contests for the prefessorial chairs,
And ordering the Faculty to grant

Padre Francisco Suarez primacy
Among the masters theological.
And Frei Egidio, whose ancient name
Fonseca was relinquished when at court
It shone its brightest, who had ceaseless toiled
His score of years in cloister and in schools,
Unravelling knotty texts, disputing long
With monk and doctor of the Carmelites,
Dominicans and Trinitarians,
Consulting with the students, visiting,
Fawning and banqueting—himself and all
His faction in the University—
Now in the iron mandate from Madrid
Saw failure blight his hopes, and Santa Cruz
Eclipsed, through imposition unforeseen
Of Suarez de Toledo—only half
A monk!—a fledgling doctor in the Schools!—
And Frei Egidio unsleeping schemed
To check the rising of this Spanish star
Within Coimbra—and his henchmen went
Stealthy and sure to sow malignant seed
To choke the Hapsburg's new autocracy.
Stately was Frei Egidio, robust,
Swarthy and smooth his cheek; his raven locks
Piling about his tonsure in a crown.
Dark flashed his eye whene'er he rose to cast
His syllogistic spear across the lists,
Where many a mighty crest Minerva-crowned
Was forced to yield, or learnt the rapier thrust

Of his *distinguo* and *non-sequiter.*
Still more he shone when in procession moved
The doctors, masters, and licentiates,
With tufted caps, and rainbow gowns, and stoles,
And ring, and book across the steeps and squares,
While gallant youths pressed round on horse or foot
Holding his robe or stirrup through the town—
The *Catedratico da Vespera.*
But now this little shrivelled man sent out
From Salamanca—Philip's paragon!—
To rule Coimbra in theology!—
One of Loyola's strange and restless band
In the Collegio de Jesus—reproach
To every gorgeous doctor in the halls.
'Twas true he hid away within his house,
Came seldom to the festival or Acts,
Nor oft asserted his high presidence
O'er Frei Egidio—in craft or scorn,
It mattered not—for Frei Egidio
Would pluck him forth; no signet of the King
Could serve him here; the doctors of the Schools
Should learn how he, Fonseca, had been wronged.
With formal placards soon they smeared the walls
Of shrine and college, telling day and hour
And place, where Doutor Frei Egidio
Da Presentacao, of the Eremites
Of Sao Agostinho, titular
Da Vespera, would his conclusions hold
"De Voluntario et Involuntario"

Against all-comers, and imprimis there,
The Doutor Padre Suarez, titular
Da Prima of Coimbra, theologue
Of the *Collegia* and *Compania*
De Jesus. From near and far they came,
And took their stated rank, and filed
Into the Hall of Acts; the Chancellor
And Rector in their robes of silk, and fur,
And velvet, and great chains and seals of state;
The Bishop, and Inquisitor, and Dean,
And Chapter, in their purple; Canonists
In green; and Jurists in their scarlet gowns;
Frei Luiz of the Chair of Holy Writ,
In black and white of the Dominicans;
Frei Manoel of the Chair of Scotus, garbed
In white and brown of Carmel; titulars
In Peter Lombard and Durandus—sons
Of Bernard, Francis and Saint Benedict.
When each in order of his ancientry
Was seated in the tribune, and below
Ranged the licentiates, and bachelors,
And, out beyond, the thousand students—gay
In plumes and ruffs, or rags and disrepair—
There entered Bacharel Frei Constantino
Citing the *obligations*; whereupon
Egidio began his argument
With exposition and arrangement clear,
And summary abrupt and crushing, as
His old experience in the courts had taught—

So free in tone and doctrine that the throng
Swayed on their benches, beating noisily
Great tomes together like the roll of drums.
Then silence for Suarez's *quodlibet*;
As half-reluctant, without emphasis,
His cold unwavering voice proposed the plan
Of his objection—When uproarious
Upon the instant, Frei Egidio
In tones of thunder shouted o'er the hall—
"*Nego majorem!*"—the scholastic world's
Unmitigated insult! How would he,
Spain's boasted theologian, reply
To Portugal's? The Jesuits around
Suarez's rostrum marvelled, whispered, turned,
And hid their faces, when they saw him bowed
Silent a moment, ere descending, calm,
He led them home across the jeering town.
Then the mad acclamations; bells of shrine
And monastery on the hills; the sweep
Of robes prelatical, the cavalcade
Of gorgeous nobles into Santa Cruz;
The blare of trumpets, and the lanterns strung
Yellow beneath the moon; the beggar throngs;
The maskers down the lanes; the nightingales
And river-songs of students wafted far
Across Mondego's Hills of Loneliness
And Meditation where Coimbra slept.
Thus triumphed Frei Egidio. But high
In the Collegio de Jesus the blow

Was red on every cheek; the Rector rose
In the community and said: "Padre
Francisco, not in fifty years have we
In our Coimbra known such sore defeat;
Tell me, I pray, had you no thought to save
Your honor and the honor of our schools—
You, boast of Rome and Salamanca's halls.—
You, to whom all the dialectic arts
Have been as play—could you not parry, feint,
Or bait Egidio until some chance
Or newer turn might save your argument?"
Suarez bowed and answered: "Better far
That we be humbled than a great man fall
To utter shame and ruin! Had I told
Egidio there that in denying thus
My proposition he was challenging
A solemn canon, word for word, prescribed
At Constance by the Universal Church—
Fetch me the Book of Councils—he was lost."
Scarce was the secret spoken, ere it stole
In rumor through the novice-court, and thence
Below to Santa Cruz—stole, like a cloud,
Black, ominous, across the starlit dome
Above the black *mosteiro*, where the moon
Revelled amid the sculptured lattices—
The marble ropes and palms memorial
Of old Da Gama and his caravels—
Upon the rose-paths and the trickling pools
Along the Cloister do Silencio.

There paced Fonseca, solitary guest
To catch the final crumbs, the laughter, far
Adown the stream, of lutes that mourned his feast,
When lo! a billet in his path!—"*Awake—*"
He read—"*at Constance 'twas decreed. Thy voice
Hath mocked the very words of Holy Church.*"—
No more—yet in foreboding he made haste
To find his taper—fumbled through the stacks
In dust and chill—unclasped the folio
Liber Conciliorum—saw his doom—
Perchance the rack and Secret Prisons—writ
Upon the parchment!—Silence, mocking lutes!
Come, rain! come, whirlwind, blot the lanterns out:
Now knew he their insidious subterfuge—
The slippery Pharisees—to undermine
Coimbra's last bright paragon—they claimed
Another victim!—But his rage gave way
To grief; his scorn was all to blame; no scheme
Was theirs; Suarez spoke the Council's words
As duty bound him—With the break of day
Came self-renouncement to Egidio;
And in amaze to greet his ashen face
The sacristan laid out for him the alb
And chasuble of Requiem; resigned,
Like some bowed reed the storm has swept by night,
He took the chalice, veiled it 'gainst his breast,
And 'mid the first faint glimmer down the nave
Crept forth unto his mystic Calvary.